BARTHOLOMEW

EDINBURGH
STREET GUIDE

ATLAS

INSIDE COVERS

Layout of map pages

John Bartholomew & Son Ltd. Edinburgh

Revised edition MCMLXXXV

© JOHN BARTHOLOMEW & SON LTD., Edinburgh
Printed and Published in Scotland by
John Bartholomew & Son Ltd. MCMLXXXV
Reprinted MCMLXXXVI
ISBN 0 7028 0294 8

B073

Scale of main map pages - 1:15 000 (4.2 inches to 1 mile)

```
0              0.5              1              1.5  km
├───────────────┼───────────────┼───────────────┤
0          ¹4          ¹2          ³4
                                                mile
```

main through road
axe principal
Durchgangsstraße

dual carriageway
chaussées séparées
Straße mit getrennten Fahrbahnen

main link road
axe secondaire
Verbindungsstraße

other roads
autres rues
sonstige Straßen

lane, drive
petite rue, allée
Gaße, Einfahrt

walkway
passage
Fußgängerweg

path
sentier
Pfad

railways
lignes ferroviaires
Eissenbahnlinien

main station
gare principale
Hauptbahnhof

airport coach station
aérogare
Abfahrt zum Flughafen

car park
parking
Parkplatz

taxi rank
station de taxi
Taxistand

tourist information centre
syndicat d'initiative
Informationsbüro

principal hotel
▲ George *hôtel important*
führendes Hotel

consulate
ⒸⒽ *consulat*
Konsulat

public building
⌐ *bâtiment public*
öffentliches Gebäude

theatre/public hall
★ King's *théâtre/salle de réunion*
Theater/Veranstaltungshalle

cinema
★ A.B.C. *cinéma*
Kino

museum or gallery
O Tolbooth *musée ou galerie d'art*
Museen

toilets
♦ ♦ *toilettes*
Toiletten

library
★ *bibliothèque*
Bibliothek

police station
Ⓟ *poste de police*
Polizeiwache

shopping centre
centre commerçant
Einkaufszentrum

dense built up area
noyau urbain
dicht bebautes Gebiet

open residential area
zone résidentielle
offen bebaute Wohnfläche

primary school
△ *école primaire*
Grundschule

secondary school
▲ *école secondaire*
Höhere Schule

church
+ *église*
Kirche

tower block
▌ *immeuble élevé*
Hochlaus

open land
terrain non loti
unbebautes Gebiet

park
jardin
Park

woodland
terrain boisé
Wald

picturesque road
route pittoresque
landschaftlich schöne Straße

viewpoint
pointe de vue
Aussichtspunkt

cemetery
cimitière
Friedhof

recreation area
terrain de sport
Sportgelände

swimming pool
〜 *piscine*
Schwimmbad

sailing centre
▲ *centre de voile*
Segelhafen

caravan camping site
🚐 ⋀ *caravaning/camping*
Campingplatz

postal boundary
EH5 *limite de district postal*
Postbezirksgrenze

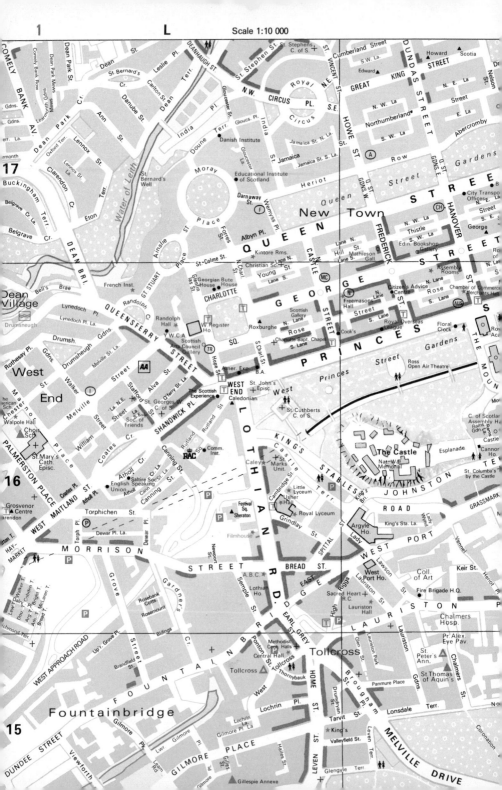

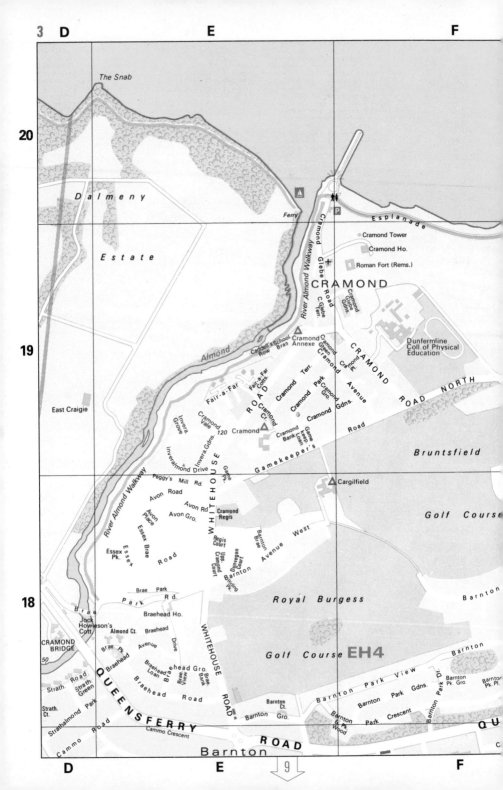

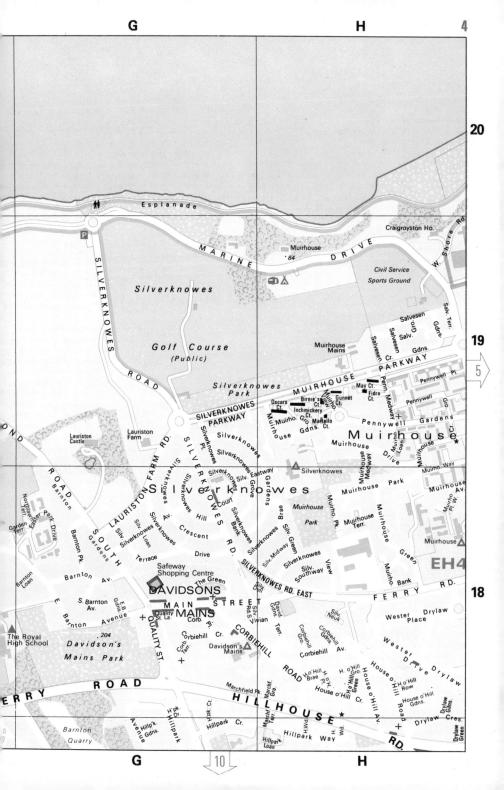

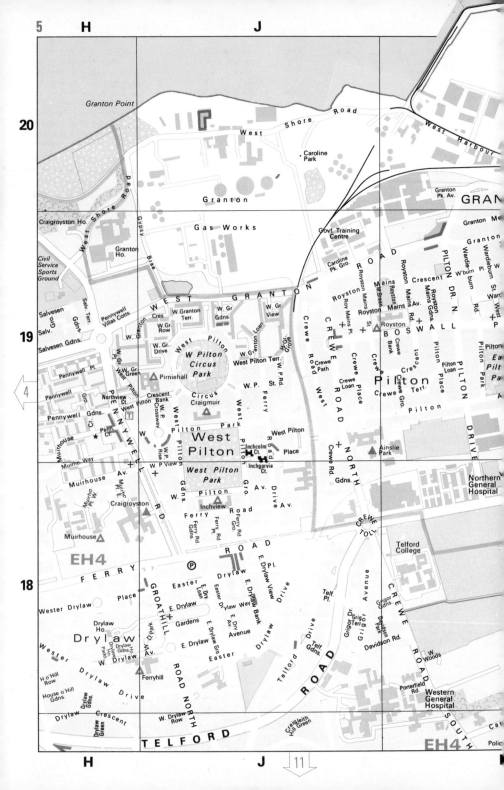

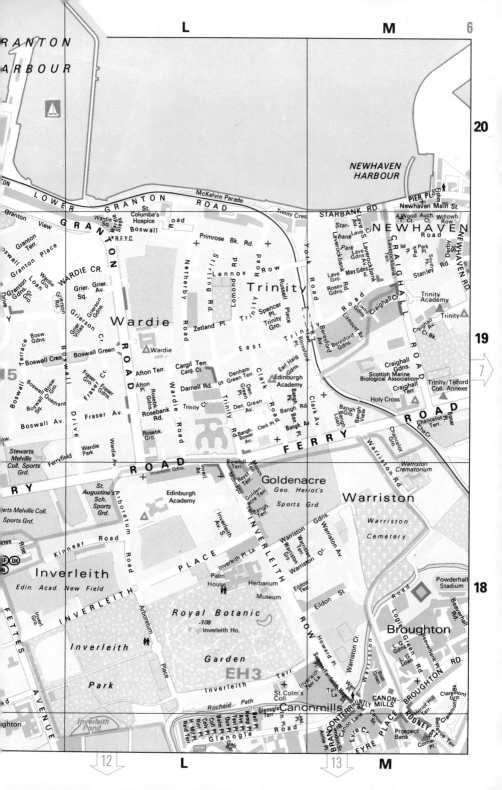

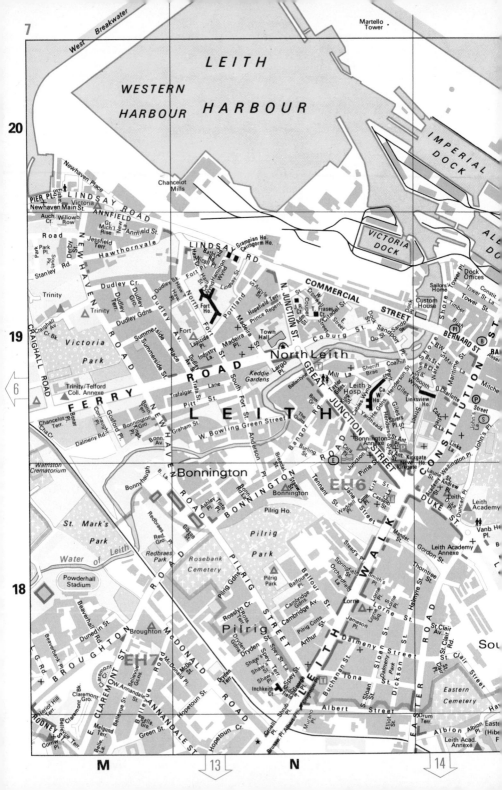

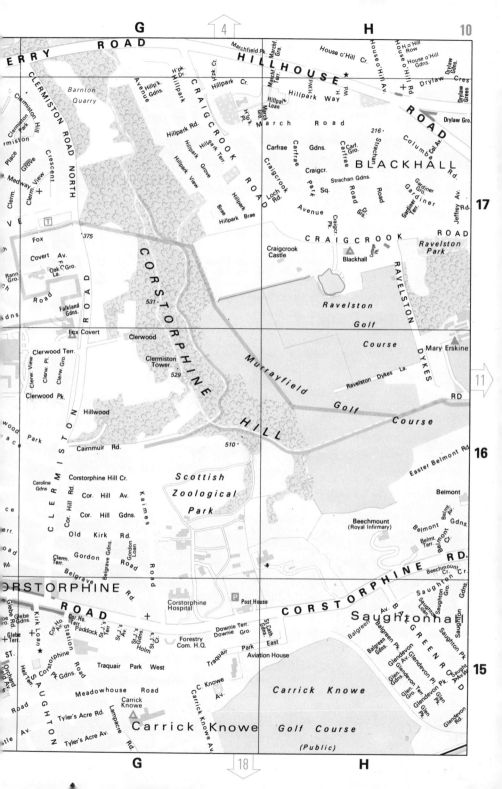

Canonmills

CANON-MILLS

Prospect Bank

King George V Park

HENDERSON ROW

BRANDON TERRACE

RODNEY PLACE

E. CLAREMONT ST.

ANNANDALE

McDONALD RD

LEITH WALK

Albert

DUNDAS STREET

GREAT KING STREET

Cumberland

Abercromby Pl.

EAST LONDON ST.

London Street

BROUGHTON

Drummond

LONDON STREET

LONDON ROAD

Royal Terrace Gardens

Royal Terrace

QUEEN STREET

GEORGE STREET

Scott. Nat. Portrait Gall. Mus. of Antiq.

YORK PL.

St. Andrew's Ho.

New St. Andrew's Ho.

Bus Sta.

Royal Bank of Scotland

LEITH ST.

GREENSIDE

CALTON

Calton Hill

City Observatory

National Mon.

Nelson's Mon.

Regent Gardens

Calton

REGENT ROAD

PRINCES STREET

Freemasons' Hall

Music Rooms

Rose St.

THE MOUND

Royal Scott. Academy

Nat. Gallery

Waverley Market

Waverley Sta.

NORTH BRIDGE

WATERLOO PL.

St. Andrew's Ho.

Crown Office Bldgs.

Calton New Burial Ground

West Princes Street Gardens

Princes Street Gardens

Market St.

BANK ST.

HIGH ST.

St Giles

Cath.

SOUTH BRIDGE

CANONGATE

Canongate

HOLYROOD RD

The Castle

JOHNSTON TERR.

Esplanade

CASTLE

GRASSMARKET

COWGATE

Heriot-Watt Univ.

CANDLEMAKER ROW

CHAMBERS ST.

Royal Scot. Museum

Edin. Univ.

PLEASANCE

Dumbiedykes

EH8

EH1

Greyfriars Kirk

George Heriot's

Coll. of Art

WEST PORT

LAURISTON PLACE

FORREST RD

Student Centre

TEVIOT PL.

BRISTO

Medical Sch.

McEwan Hall

NICOLSON STREET

Surgeons Hall

Deaconess Hospital

Chalmers Hosp.

Royal Infirmary

George Sq.

Univ. Library

BUCCLEUCH ST.

Crosscauseway

St. Leonards

Toll-cross

HOME ST.

Simpson Meml. Maternity Pavilion

North Meadow Walk

The Meadows

Middle Meadow Walk

CLERK ST.

St. LEONARDS ST.

DALKEITH RD

Bruntsfield

Bruntsfield Links

MELVILLE DRIVE

MARCHMONT RD

Royal Hosp. for Sick Children

HOPE PARK TERR.

Royal (Dick) Vet. Coll.

PRESTON ST.

Salisbury

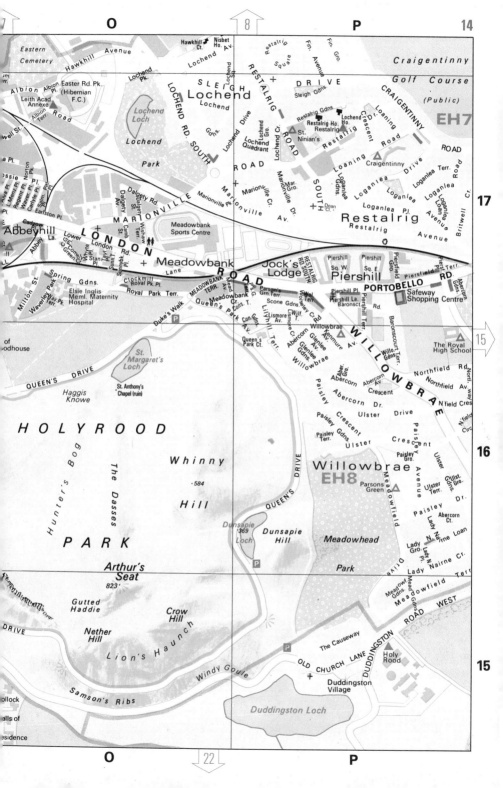

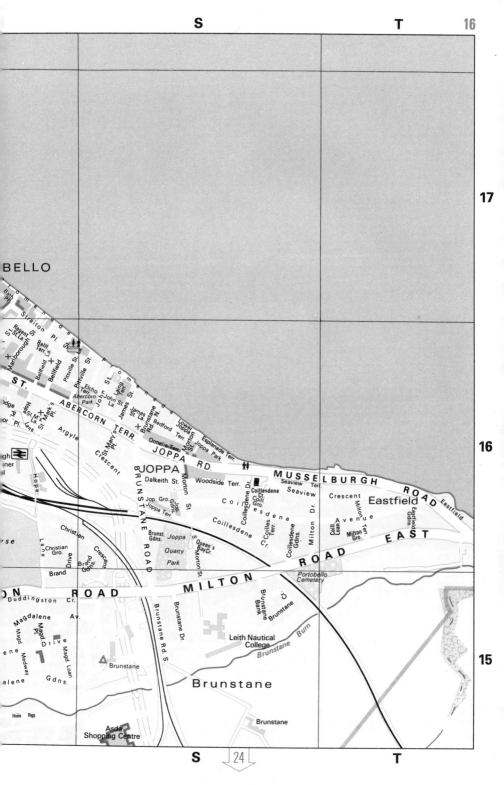

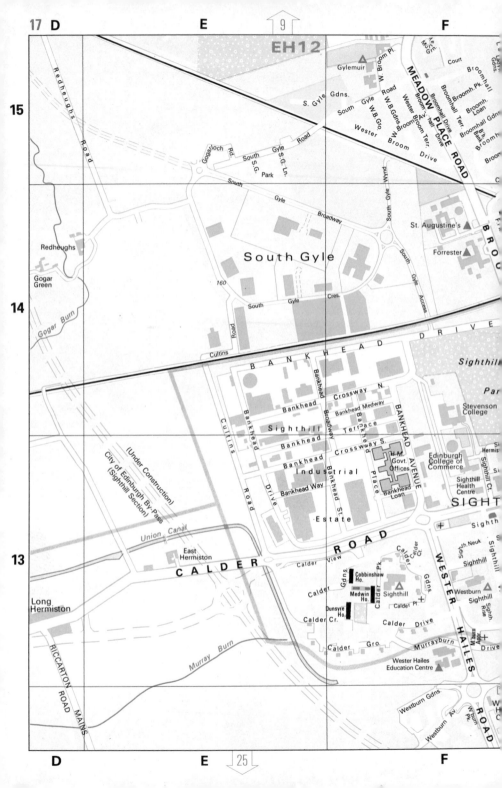

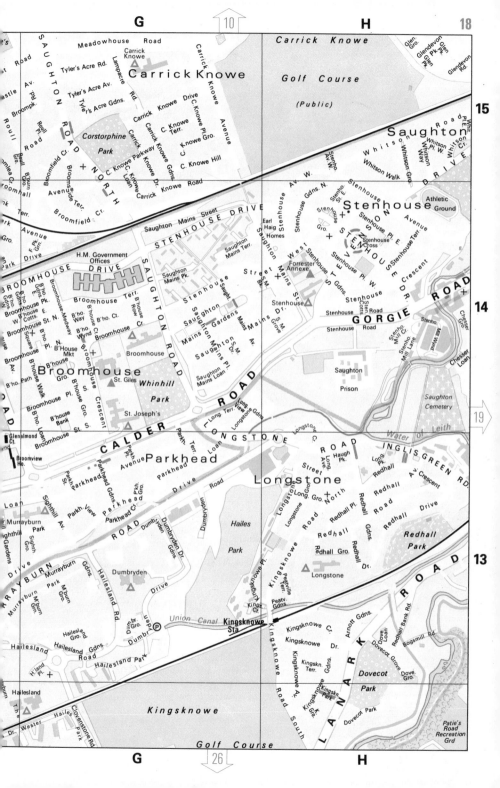

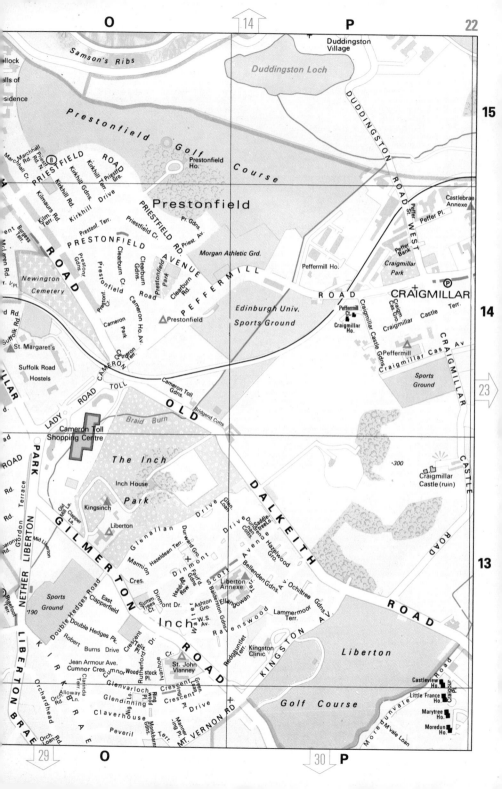

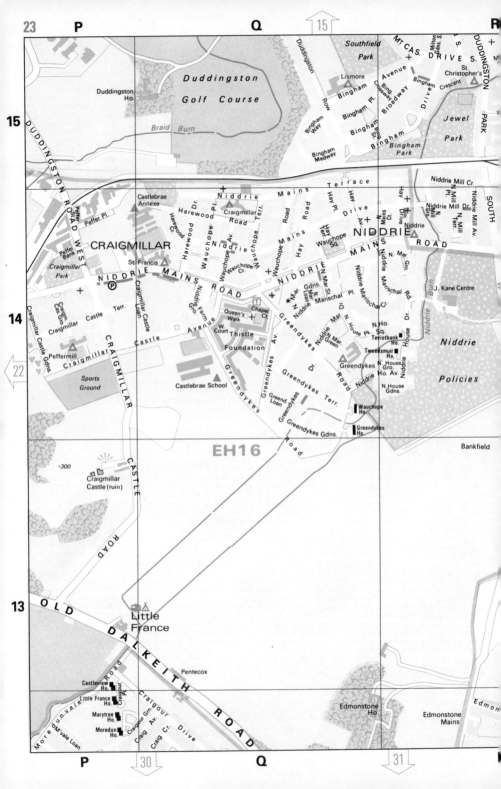

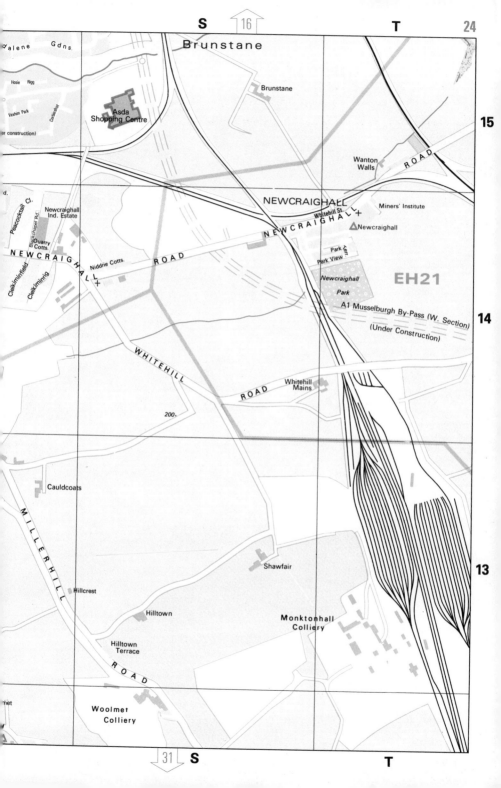

Brunstane

valene Gdns.

Hosie Rigg

Brunstane

Vexhim Park

Carlawhur

er construction)

Asda
Shopping Centre

Wanton
Walls

ROAD

NEWCRAIGHALL

Miners' Institute

Peacocktail Cl.

Newcraighall
Ind. Estate

Whitehill St.

NEWCRAIGHALL

△Newcraighall

Quarry
Cotts.

Blackchapel Rd.

Cleikiminfield

Cleikimining

NEWCRAIGHALL

Niddrie Cotts.

ROAD

Park Terr.

Park View

Newcraighall

Park

EH21

A1 Musselburgh By-Pass (W. Section)

(Under Construction)

WHITEHILL

ROAD

Whitehill
Mains

200.

MILLERHILL

Cauldcoats

Hillcrest

Shawfair

Hilltown

Monktonhall
Colliery

Hilltown
Terrace

ROAD

net

Woolmet
Colliery

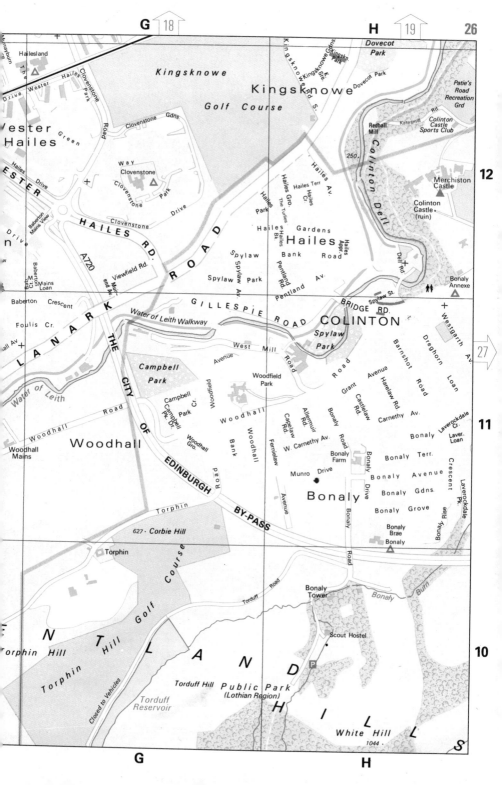

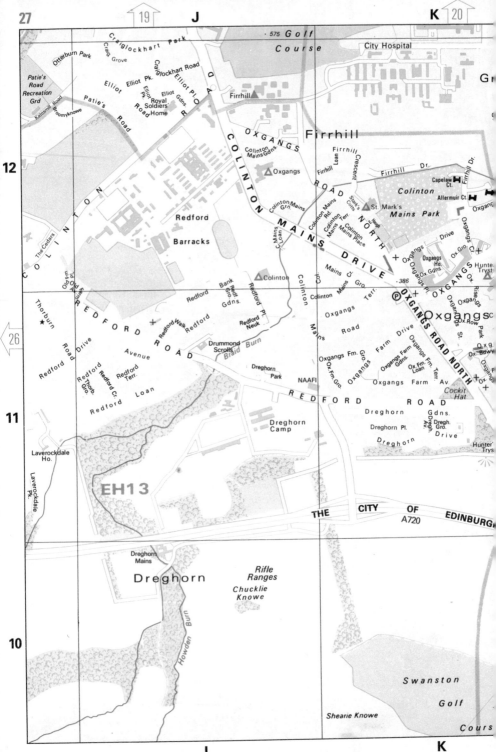

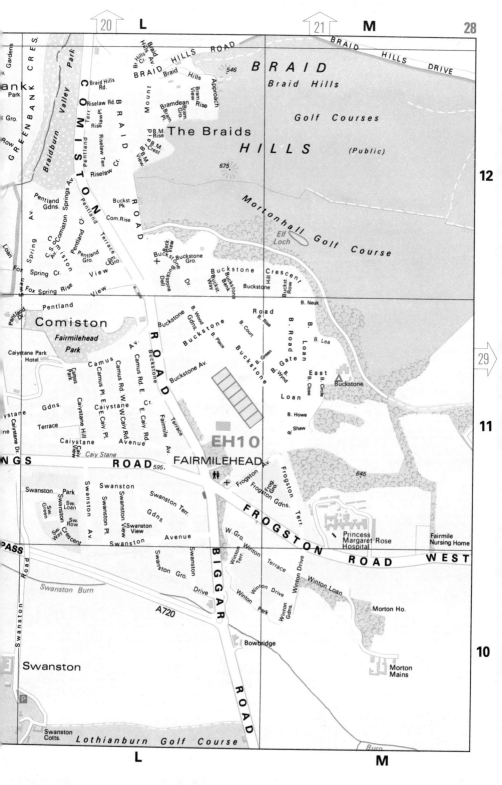

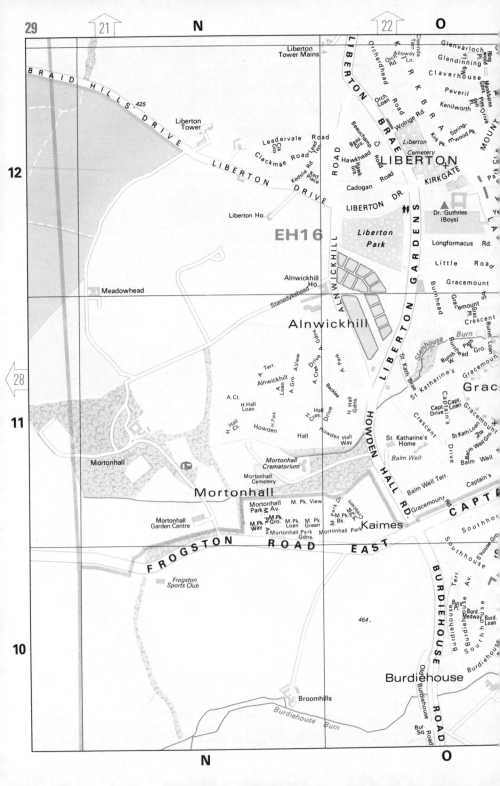

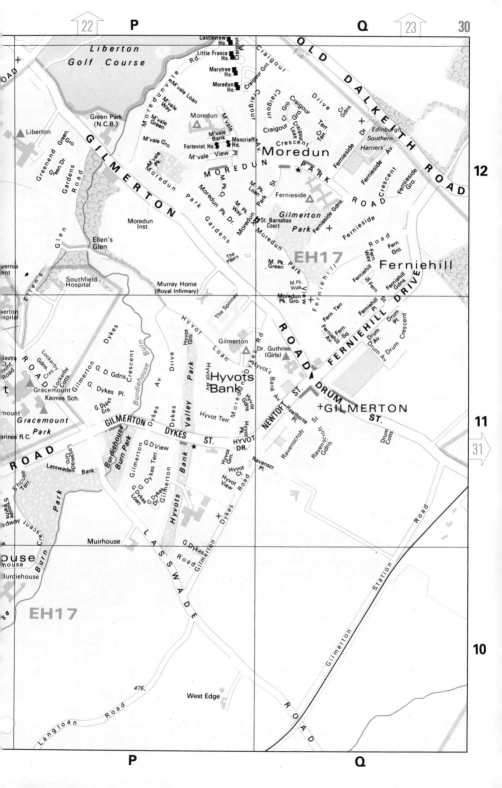

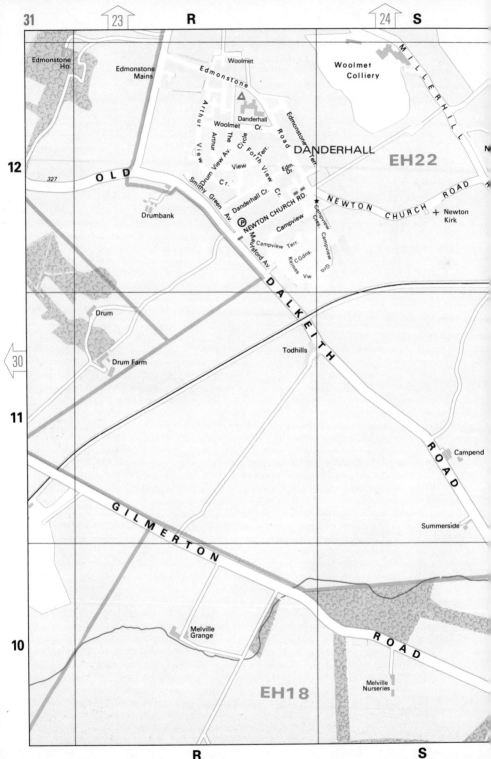

Edmonstone
Ho.

Edmonstone
Mains

Woolmet

Woolmet
Colliery

Edmonstone

Danderhall
Cr.

Woolmet

Arthur
View

Arthur
Cr.

The
Ci'rcle

Drum View Av.

Forth
View

Edmonstone Terr.

Road

DANDERHALL

EH22

12

327

OLD

Smithy Green Av.

Danderhall Cr.

Cr.

Edm.
Dt.

NEWTON CHURCH RD.

NEWTON CHURCH ROAD

✦ Newton
Kirk

Drumbank

Ⓟ

Maysford Av.

Campview

Campview Terr.

Campview Cres.

Campview Gro.

Kames
CGdns.

Vw

+ Newton
Kirk

DALKEITH

Drum

Drum Farm

Todhills

11

ROAD

Campend

Summerside

GILMERTON

Melville
Grange

10

EH18

ROAD

Melville
Nurseries

← 30

Abbreviations
Acad. — Academy
Appr. — Approach
Av. — Avenue
Bdgs. — Buildings
Bdwy. — Broadway
Bk. — Bank
Cem. — Cemetery
Cl. — Close
Coll. — College
Cotts. — Cottages
Cr. — Crescent
Crem. — Crematorium
Ct. — Court
Dr. — Drive
E. — East
Er. — Easter
Fm. — Farm
Gall. — Gallery
Gdn. — Garden
Gdns. — Gardens
Gr. — Green
Grd. — Ground
Gro. — Grove
Ho. — House
Hosp. — Hospital
La. — Lane
Ln. — Loan
Lo. — Lodge
Mem. — Memorial
N. — North
Pav. — Pavilion
Pk. — Park
Pl. — Place
Pt. — Port
Qt. — Quadrant
Rd. — Road
S. — South
Sch. — School
Sq. — Square
St. — Saint, Street
Sta. — Station
Terr. — Terrace
Vw. — View
W. — West
Wr. — Wester
Wy. — Way

An asterisk in the index indicates a street too small to show on the plan and an equals sign refers to the nearest street name.

14 Abbey La. **O17**
14 Abbey St. **O17**
2 Abbey Strand **N16**
2 Abbeyhill **N16**
13 Abbeyhill Cr. **N17**
14 Abbeyhill Sch. **O17**
2 Abbeymount **N17**
20 Abbotsford Cr. **L14**
20 Abbotsford Cr. **L14**
20 Abbotsford Park **L14**
1 ABC Cinema **L16**
14 Abercorn Avenue **P16**
Abercorn Cotts.* = The Causeway
14 Abercorn Ct. **P16**
14 Abercorn Dr. **P16**
14 Abercorn Dr. **P16**
15 Abercorn Gdns. **P17**
14 Abercorn Gro. **P16**
16 Abercorn Park **S16**
14 Abercorn Rd. **P16**
16 Abercorn Terr. **R16**
1 Abercromby Pl. **M17**
11 Abinger Gdns. **J16**
7 Academy Street **O18**
2 Accommodation Bureau **M16**
2 Adam House **M16**
15 Adelphi Gro. **R16**
15 Adelphi Pl. **R16**
20 Admiral Terr. **L15**
7 Admiralty St. **N19**
Advocates Cl.* = High St.
6 Afton Pl. **L19**

6 Afton Terr. **L19**
Agnew Terr.* = Connaught Pl.
5 Ainslie Park Sch. **J19**
1 Ainslie Pl. **L17**
2 Air Terminal **M16**
12 Airlie Pl. **M17**
Aitchison's Pl.* = Figgate St.
9 Alan Breck Gdns. **F17**
2 Albany La. **M17**
2 Albany St. **M17**
2 Albany St. La. **M17**
13 Albert Pl. **N17**
8 Albert Road **O19**
7 Albert St. **N18**
20 Albert Terr. **L14**
14 Albion Pl. **O17**
14 Albion Rd. **O17**
14 Albion Terr. **O17**
1 Albyn Pl. **L17**
19 Alderbank Gdns. **K14**
19 Alderbank Pl. **K14**
19 Alderbank Terr. **K14**
15 Alexander Dr. **J15**
21 Alfred Pl. **N14**
19 Allan Park Cr. **J14**
19 Allan Park Dr. **J13**
19 Allan Park Gdns. **J13**
19 Allan Park Loan **J13**
19 Allan Park Rd. **J13**
12 Allan St. **L17**
27 Allermuir Ct. **K12**
26 Allermuir Rd. **H11**
29 Alloway Loan **O12**
3 Almond Ct. **E18**
3 Almond Gr. **E16**
9 Almond Sq. **E16**
Almondbank Cotts.* = Whitehouse Rd.
19 Almondbank Terr. **K14**
29 Alnwickhill Cr. **N11**
29 Alnwickhill Gdns **O11**
29 Alnwickhill Gro. **N11**
29 Alnwickhill Loan **N11**
29 Alnwickhill Pk. **O11**
29 Alnwickhill Rd. **O12**
29 Alnwickhill Terr. **N11**
29 Alnwickhill View **N11**
14 Alva Pl. **O17**
3 Alva St. **L16**
Alvanley Terr.* = Whitehouse Loan
1 American Sch, The **L16**
Anchorfield* = Lindsay Rd.
7 Anderson Pl. **N19**
6 Andrew Wood Ct. **M19**
12 Angle Park Terr. **K15**
1 Ann St. **L17**
3 Annandale St. **M18**
13 Annandale St. La. **N17**
7 Annfield **M19**
7 Annfield St. **M19**
2 Antigua St. **N17**
8 Appin Terr. **J14**
2 Appleton Tower **M15**
12 Arboretum Av. **L17**
6 Arboretum Rd. **L18**
6 Arboretum Pl. **L18**
2 Archer's Hall **N15**
1 Archibald Pl. **M16**
21 Arden St. **M15**
20 Ardmillan Pl. **K15**
20 Ardmillan Terr. **K15**
Ardmillan Terr. La.* = Ardmillan Terr.
9 Ardshiel Av. **F17**
16 Argyle Cr. **R16**
1 Argyle House **M16**
13 Argyle Park Terr. **M15**
13 Argyle Pl. **M15**
7 Argyle St. **N19**
1 Argyll Terr. **L16**
18 Arnott Gdns. **H13**
17 Arthur St. **N18**
31 Arthur View Cr. **R12**
31 Arthur View Terr. **R12**
14 Arthur's Seat **O15**

16 Asda Shopping Centre **S15**
21 Ashfield **M14**
19 Ashley Dr. **K14**
19 Ashley Gdns. **K14**
19 Ashley Gro. **K14**
7 Ashley Pl. **N18**
19 Ashley Terr. **K14**
22 Ashton Gro. **O13**
Ashton Villas* = Brunstane Rd.
8 Ashville Terr. **O18**
1 Assembly Hall **M16**
1 Assembly Rooms **M16**
7 Assembly St. **O19**
20 Astley Ainslie Hosp. **M14**
1 Atholl Cr. **L16**
1 Atholl Cr. La. **L16**
1 Atholl Pl. **L16**
1 Atholl Terr. **L16**
6 Auchinleck Ct. **M19**
Auchinleck's Brae* = Main St.
Avenue Villas* = Crewe Rd.
10 Aviation Ho. **G15**
3 Avon Gr. **E18**
3 Avon Pl. **E18**
3 Avon Rd. **E18**
12 Avondale Pl. **L17**

25 Baberton Av. **F11**
26 Baberton Cr. **F11**
25 Baberton Golf Course **E11**
25 Baberton Loan **F11**
25 Baberton Mains Bk. **F12**
25 Baberton Mains Brae **F12**
26 Baberton Mains Ct. **G12**
25 Baberton Mains Cr. **F12**
25 Baberton Mains Dell **F12**
25 Baberton Mains Dr. **F12**
25 Baberton Mains Gdns. **F12**
25 Baberton Mains Gr. **F12**
25 Baberton Mains Gro. **F12**
25 Baberton Mains Hill **F12**
25 Baberton Mains Lea **F12**
26 Baberton Mains Loan **G12**
25 Baberton Mains Park **F12**
25 Baberton Mains Rise **F12**
25 Baberton Mains Row **F12**
25 Baberton Mains Terr. **F12**
26 Baberton Mains View **G12**
25 Baberton Mains Way **F12**
25 Baberton Mains Wood **F12**
25 Baberton Mains Wynd **F12**
25 Baberton Park **F11**
25 Baberton Sq. **F11**
12 Back Dean **K17**
29 Backlea **O11**
Back Station Rd.* = Peffer St.
17 Baileyfield Rd. **Q17**
16 Bailie Gro. **R15**
16 Bailie Path **R15**
16 Bailie Pl. **R15**
15 Bailie Terr. **R15**
11 Baird Av. **J15**
11 Baird Dr. **J15**
11 Baird Gdns. **J15**
11 Baird Gro. **J15**
11 Baird Terr. **J15**
Baker's Pl.* = Kerr St.
11 Balbirnie Pl. **K16**
20 Balcarres Ct. **L13**
20 Balcarres St. **K13**
22 Balderston Gdns. **O13**

7 Balfour Pl. **N18**
7 Balfour St. **N18**
9 Balfron Loan **F17**
10 Balgreen Av. **H15**
10 Balgreen Gdns. **H15**
10 Balgreen Park **H15**
10 Balgreen Rd. **H15**
19 Balgreen Sch. **J15**
7 Ballantyne Rd. **N19**
29 Balm Well Av. **O11**
29 Balm Well Gro. **O11**
29 Balm Well Pk. **O11**
29 Balm Well Terr. **O11**
12 Balmoral Pl. **L17**
7 Baltic St. **O19**
6 Bangholm Av. **L19**
6 Bangholm Bower Av. **L19**
6 Bangholm Gro. **M19**
6 Bangholm Loan **M19**
6 Bangholm Pk. **L19**
6 Bangholm Pl. **L19**
6 Bangholm Rd. **L19**
6 Bangholm Terr. **L18**
6 Bangholm View **M19**
Bangholm Villas* = Ferry Rd.
9 Bangor Rd. **N19**
2 Bank of Scotland **M16**
2 Bank St. **M16**
17 Bankhead Av. **F14**
17 Bankhead Bdwy. **E14**
17 Bankhead Crossway N. **E14**
17 Bankhead Crossway S.**E13**
17 Bankhead Dr. **E14,F14**
17 Bankhead Loan **F13**
17 Bankhead Medway **F14**
17 Bankhead Pl. **F14**
17 Bankhead St. **F13**
17 Bankhead Terr. **E13**
17 Bankhead Way **E13**
Barclay Pl.* = Bruntsfield Pl.
20 Barclay Terr. **L15**
26 Barnshot Rd. **H11**
3 Barnton Av. **F18**
3 Barnton Av. E. **G18**
3 Barnton Av. W. **E18**
9 Barnton Brae **E18**
9 Barnton Ct. **E18**
4 Barnton Gdns **G18**
4 Barnton Gro. **E18**
4 Barnton Loan **G18**
4 Barnton Park **G18**
3 Barnton Park Av. **F18**
3 Barnton Park Cr. **F18**
9 Barnton Park Dell **F18**
9 Barnton Park Dr. **F18**
9 Barnton Park Gdns. **F18**
3 Barnton Park Gro. **F18**
3 Barnton Park Pl. **F18**
9 Barnton Park View **F18**
9 Barnton Park Wood **E17**
9 Barntongate Av. **E17**
3 Barntongate Dr. **E17**
9 Barntongate Terr. **E17**
14 Baronscourt Rd. **P17**
14 Baronscourt Terr. **P17**
2 Barony Pl. **M17**
2 Barony St. **M17**
9 Barony Terr. **F16**
9 Barony Terr. W. **F16**
16 Bath Pl. **R17**
8 Bath Rd. **O19**
15 Bath St. **R16**
Bath St. La.* = Bath St.
7 Bathfield Rd. **N19**
Baxter's Pl.* = Leith Walk
15 Beach Lane **R17**
29 Beauchamp Gro. **O12**
29 Beauchamp Rd. **O12**
21 Beaufort Rd. **M14**

2 Beaumont Pl. N15
6 Beaverbank Pl. M18
7 Beaverhall Rd. M18
12 Bedford Cr. L17
12 Bedford Ct. L17
12 Bedford St. L17
16 Bedford Terr. S16
12 Beechmount H16
10 Beechmount Cr. H16
8 Beechwood Terr. O18
12 Belford Av. K17
12 Belford Gdns. K17
12 Belford Mews K16
12 Belford Park K16
12 Belford Pl. K17
12 Belford Rd. K16
Belford Terr.* =
  Belford Rd.
12 Belgrave Cr. K17
12 Belgrave Cr. La. K17
10 Belgrave Gdns. G16
12 Belgrave Mews K17
12 Belgrave Pl. K17
10 Belgrave Rd. G16
Belgrave Terr.* =
  Clermiston Rd.
20 Belhaven Terr. L13
12 Bell Pl. L17
22 Bellenden Gdns. P13
13 Bellevue M17
13 Bellevue Cr. M17
13 Bellevue Gdns. M18
13 Bellevue Gro. M17
13 Bellevue La. M17
13 Bellevue Pl. M17
13 Bellevue Rd. M17
13 Bellevue St. M17
13 Bellevue Terr. M17
16 Bellfield La. R16
16 Bellfield St. R16
16 Bellfield Terr. R16
1 Bells Brae L16
Bell's Mills* = Belford Rd.
Bell's Wynd* = High St.
10 Belmont Av. H16
10 Belmont Cr. H16
10 Belmont Gdns. H16
10 Belmont Park H16
25 Belmont Rd. F11
10 Belmont Terr. H16
11 Belmont View H16
6 Belvedere Park M19
6 Beresford Av. M19
6 Beresford Gdns. M19
6 Beresford Pl. L19
6 Beresford Terr. M19
7 Bernard St. O19
2 Bernard Terr. N15
Berry Sq.* = Figgate
  St., Portobello
28 Biggar Rd. L11
15 Bingham Av. Q15
23 Bingham Bdwy. Q15
23 Bingham Cr. R15
23 Bingham Crossway R15
23 Bingham Dr. Q15
23 Bingham Medway Q15
23 Bingham Park R15
23 Bingham Pl. Q15
23 Bingham St. Q15
23 Bingham Way Q15
9 Birch Ct. E17
1 Birnie's Ct. H19
21 Blacket Av. N15
21 Blacket Pl. N15
22 Blackbarony Rd. O13
24 Blackchapel Rd. R14
21 Blackford Av. M14
21 Blackford Bk. M14
21 Blackford Glen Rd. N13
21 Blackford Hill M13
21 Blackford Hill Gro. M13
21 Blackford Hill Rise M13
21 Blackford Hill View M13
21 Blackford Rd. M14
2 Blackfriars St. N16
10 Blackhall Sch. H17
8 Blackie Rd. O18

17 Blackthorn Ct. E17
21 Blackwood Cr. N15
17 Blaeberry Gdns. E17
13 Blair St. M16
20 Blantyre Terr. L14
2 Blenheim Pl. N17
11 Blinkbonny Av. J17
11 Blinkbonny Cr. J17
11 Blinkbonny Gdns. J17
11 Blinkbonny Gro. J17
11 Blinkbonny Gro. W. J17
11 Blinkbonny Rd. J17
25 Blinkbonny Rd., Currie
  E10
11 Blinkbonny Terr. J17
25 Bloomiehall Park F11
6 Boat Green M18
18 Bogsmill Rd. H13
26 Bonaly Av. H11
26 Bonaly Brae H11
26 Bonaly Cr. H11
26 Bonaly Dr. H11
26 Bonaly Farm H11
26 Bonaly Gdns. H11
26 Bonaly Gro. H11
26 Bonaly Rise H11
26 Bonaly Rd. H11
26 Bonaly Sch. H10
26 Bonaly Sch. Annexe H12
26 Bonaly Terr. H11
7 Bonar Pl. M19
7 Bonnington Av. M19
7 Bonnington Gro. M19
7 Bonnington Rd. N18
7 Bonnington Rd. La. M18
7 Bonnington Sch. N18
7 Bonnington Sch. Annexe
  N19
7 Bonnington Terr. M19
7 Bonnyhaugh M18
7 Bonnyhaugh La. M18
Boothacre Cotts.* =
  Seafield Pl.
8 Boothacre La. P18
Boroughloch Bdgs.* =
  Boroughloch Sq.
2 Boroughloch La. N15
Boroughloch Sq.* =
  Boroughloch La.
12 Boroughmuir Sch. L15
12 Boroughmuir Sch.
  Annexe L15
12 Borthwick Pl. K16
Borthwick's Cl.* = High St.
6 Boswall Av. K19
6 Boswall Cr. K19
6 Boswall Dr. K19
6 Boswall Gdns. K19
6 Boswall Gr. L19
6 Boswall Gro. K19
6 Boswall Loan K19
5 Boswall Parkway K19
6 Boswall Pl. K19
6 Boswall Qt. K19
6 Boswall Rd. L19
6 Boswall Sq. K19
6 Boswall Terr. K19
18 Bothwell St. O17
6 Bowhill Terr. L18
Bowie's Cl. O19
7 Bowling Green, The N19
3 Brae Park E18
3 Brae Park Rd. D18
22 Braefoot Terr. O13
3 Braehead Av. E18
3 Braehead Bank E18
3 Braehead Drive E18
3 Braehead Gro. E18
3 Braehead Loan E18
3 Braehead Pk. E18
3 Braehead Rd. E18
3 Braehead View E18
20 Braid Av. L13
20 Braid Cr. L13
20 Braid Farm Rd. L13
29 Braid Hills M12
20 Braid Hills Approach L12
20 Braid Hills Av. L13

20 Braid Hills Cr. L12
21 Braid Hills Dr. M13
28 Braid Hills Golf Course
  M12
28 Braid Hills Rd. L12
28 Braid Mount L12
28 Braid Mt. Crest L12
28 Braid Mt. Rise L12
28 Braid Mt. View L12
28 Braid Rd. L12
28 Braidburn Cr. L13
28 Braidburn Terr. L13
28 Braidburn Valley Park
  L12
9 Bramble Dr. E17
28 Bramdean Gro. L12
28 Bramdean Pl. L12
28 Bramdean Rise L12
28 Bramdean View L12
17 Brand Dr. R15
17 Brand Gdns. R15
Brand Pl.* = Abbeyhill
1 Brandfield St. L15
13 Brandon St. M17
13 Brandon Terr. M17
1 Bread St. L16
Bread St. La.* =
  Bread St.
12 Bread Terr. L16
1 Breadalbane St. N19
1 Breadalbane Terr. L16
7 Brewery La. N19
19 Briarbank Terr. K14
Brickwork Cl.* = Giles St.
12 Bridge Pl. L17
26 Bridge Rd. H11
15 Bridge St. R17
15 Bridge St. La. R17
22 Bridgend Cotts. O14
1 Bright Terr. L16
15 Brighton Park R16
15 Brighton Pl. R16
2 Brighton St. M16
21 Bright's Cr. N14
2 Bristo Pl. M16
2 Bristo Port M16
2 Bristo Sq. M16
2 Bristo St. M16
21 British Geological Survey
  M14, N13
15 Britwell Cr. P17
7 Broad Wynd O19
18 Broombank Terr. F14
18 Broombarn Gro. G15
18 Broomfield Cr. G14
18 Broomhall Av. F15
17 Broomhall Bank F15
17 Broomhall Cr. F15
17 Broomhall Dr. F15
17 Broomhall Gdns. F15
17 Broomhall Loan F15
17 Broomhall Park F15
17 Broomhall Pl. F15
17 Broomhall Rd. F15
17 Broomhall Terr. F15
29 Broomhills M10
18 Broomhouse Av. F14
18 Broomhouse Bank F14
18 Broomhouse Cotts. E.
  G14
18 Broomhouse Cotts. W.
  F14
18 Broomhouse Ct. G14
18 Broomhouse Cr. G14
18 Broomhouse Dr. F14
18 Broomhouse Gdns. F14
18 Broomhouse Gdns. E. G14
18 Broomhouse Gdns. W.
  F14
18 Broomhouse Gro. G14
18 Broomhouse Loan G14
18 Broomhouse Market G14
18 Broomhouse Medway G14
18 Broomhouse Park F14
18 Broomhouse Path F14
18 Broomhouse Pl. N. F14
18 Broomhouse Pl. S. G14
18 Broomhouse Row G14

18 Broomhouse Sch. G14
18 Broomhouse Sq. G14
18 Broomhouse St. N. F14
18 Broomhouse St. S. G13
18 Broomhouse Terr. F14
18 Broomhouse Walk G14
18 Broomhouse Way G14
18 Broomhouse Wynd G14
18 Broomlea Cr. F15
18 Broompark Rd. F15
18 Broomside Terr. G15
18 Broomview House F13
27 Broomyknowe H12
1 Brougham Pl. M15
1 Brougham St. L15
2 Broughton Market M17
13 Broughton Pl. M17
7 Broughton Rd. M18
7 Broughton Sch. M18
12 Broughton Sch. (Sec.)
  K17
2 Broughton St. M17
2 Broughton St. La. M17
Brown's Cl.* = Canongate
Brown's Pl.* = Vennel
20 Bruce St. L13
16 Brunstane Bank S15
16 Brunstane Cr. S15
16 Brunstane Dr. S15
16 Brunstane Gdns. S16
16 Brunstane Rd. S16
16 Brunstane Rd. N. S16
16 Brunstane Rd. S. S15
16 Brunstane Sch. S15
13 Brunswick Pl. N17
13 Brunswick Rd. N17
13 Brunswick St. N17
13 Brunswick St. La. N17
Brunton Gdns.* =
  Montgomery St.
13 Brunton Pl. N17
13 Brunton Terr. N17
20 Bruntsfield Av. L15
21 Bruntsfield Cr. L15
20 Bruntsfield Gdns. L15
3 Bruntsfield Golf Course
  F19
20 Bruntsfield Hosp. L15
21 Bruntsfield Links L15
20 Bruntsfield Pl. L15
20 Bruntsfield Sch. L15
20 Bruntsfield Terr. L15
15 Bryce Av. Q17
25 Bryce Cr. E11
Bryce Gdns.* = Bryce Rd.
15 Bryce Gro. Q17
25 Bryce Pl. E11
25 Bryce Rd. E11
20 Bryson Rd. K15
2 Buccleuch Pl. M15
2 Buccleuch St. N15
2 Buccleuch Terr. N15
7 Buchanan St. N18
12 Buckingham Terr. K17
28 Buckstane Park L12
28 Buckstone Av. L11
28 Buckstone Bank L12
28 Buckstone Circle M11
28 Buckstone Cl. M11
28 Buckstone Ct. L11
28 Buckstone Cr. L12
28 Buckstone Dell L12
28 Buckstone Dr. L12
28 Buckstone Gdns. L11
28 Buckstone Gate M11
28 Buckstone Gr. L11
28 Buckstone Gro L12
28 Buckstone Hill L12
28 Buckstone Howe M11
28 Buckstone Lea M11
28 Buckstone Loan E. M11
28 Buckstone Neuk M11
28 Buckstone Pl. L11
28 Buckstone Rise M11
28 Buckstone Rd. L11
28 Buckstone Row M12
28 Buckstone Sch. M11
28 Buckstone Shaw M11

28 Buckstone Terr. **L11**
28 Buckstone View **L12**
28 Buckstone Way **L12**
28 Buckstone Wood **L11**
28 Buckstone Wynd **M11**
9 Bughtlin Dr. **E17**
9 Bughtlin Gdns. **E16**
9 Bughtlin Gr. **E16**
9 Bughtlin Ln. **E16**
9 Bughtlin Market **E16**
9 Bughtlin Pk **E16**
9 Bughtlin Pl. **E16**
2 Bull's Cl. **N16**
29 Burdiehouse Av. **O10**
30 Burdiehouse Burn Park **P10**
30 Burdiehouse Cr. **O10**
29 Burdiehouse Crossway **O10**
29 Burdiehouse Dr. **O10**
29 Burdiehouse Loan **O10**
29 Burdiehouse Medway **O10**
29 Burdiehouse Pl. **O10**
29 Burdiehouse Rd. **O10**
30 Burdiehouse Sch. **O10**
29 Burdiehouse Sq. **O10**
29 Burdiehouse St. **O10**
29 Burdiehouse Terr. **O10**
7 Burgess St. **O19**
22 Burgess Terr. **O14**
7 Burlington St. **N19**
9 Burnbrae **E16**
29 Burnhead Cr. **O11**
29 Burnhead Gro. **O11**
29 Burnhead Loan **O11**
29 Burnhead Path E. **O11**
29 Burnhead Path W. **O11**
9 Burnside **E16**
2 Bus Sta. **M17**

7 Cables Wynd **N19**
7 Cables Wynd Ho. **N19**
3 Caddell's Row **E19**
7 Cadiz St. **O19**
23 Cadogan Rd. **O12**
14 Cadzow Pl. **O17**
27 Caerketton Ct. **K12**
13 Cairn Hotel **N17**
7 Cairngorm House **N19**
10 Cairnmuir Rd. **G16**
19 Cairnpark Sch. **H13**
28 Caiy Stane **L11**
28 Caiystane Av. **L11**
28 Caiystane Cr. **L11**
28 Caiystane Dr. **K11**
28 Caiystane Gdns. **K11**
28 Caiystane Hill **L11**
28 Caiystane Terr. **K11**
28 Caiystane View **L11**
17 Calder Ct. **F13**
17 Calder Cr. **E13**
17 Calder Dr. **F13**
17 Calder Gdns. **E13**
17 Calder Gro. **F13**
17 Calder Park **F13**
17 Calder Pl. **F13**
17 Calder Rd. **E13**
17 Calder View **E13**
12 Caledonian Cr. **K15**
1 Caledonian Hotel **L16**
12 Caledonian Pl. **K15**
12 Caledonian Rd. **L15**
1 Caley Cinema **L16**
2 Calton Hill **N17**
2 Calton Hill (Street) **N17**
2 Calton New Burial Ground **N17**
2 Calton Rd. **N16**
7 Cambridge Av. **N18**
7 Cambridge Gdns. **N18**
1 Cambridge St. **L16**
1 Cambridge St. La. **L16**
14 Cambusnethan St. **O17**
22 Cameron Cr. **O14**
22 Cameron Ho. Av **O14**
22 Cameron Park **O14**

22 Cameron Terr. **O14**
22 Cameron Toll Gdns. **O14**
22 Cameron Toll Shopping Centre **O14**
9 Cammo Bank **E17**
9 Cammo Brae **E17**
9 Cammo Cr. **E17**
9 Cammo Gdns. **E17**
9 Cammo Gro. **D17**
9 Cammo Hill **D17**
9 Cammo Parkway **E17**
9 Cammo Pl. **E17**
9 Cammo Rd. **D17**
9 Cammo Walk **D17**
11 Campbell Av. **J16**
26 Campbell Park. **G11**
26 Campbell Park Cr. **G11**
26 Campbell Park Dr. **G11**
26 Campbell Rd. **J16**
Campbell's Cl.* = Canongate
31 Campview **R12**
31 Campview Cr. **R12**
31 Campview Gdns. **R12**
31 Campview Gro. **S12**
31 Campview Terr. **R12**
28 Camus Av. **L11**
28 Camus Park **L11**
28 Camus Pl. E. **L11**
28 Camus Rd. E. **L11**
28 Camus Rd. W. **L11**
20 Canaan La. **L14**
2 Candlemaker Row **M16**
1 Canning St. **L16**
1 Canning St. La. **L16**
7 Cannon St. **N19**
7 Cannon Wynd **N19**
13 Canon La. **M17**
13 Canon St. **M17**
2 Canongate **N16**
13 Canonmills **M18**
27 Capelaw Ct. **K12**
26 Capelaw Rd. **H11**
29 Captain's Dr. **O11**
29 Captain's Loan **O11**
29 Captain's Rd. **O11**
29 Captain's Row **O11**
11 Carberry Pl. **K16**
10 Carfrae Gdns. **H17**
11 Carfrae Gro. **H17**
11 Carfrae Park **H17**
11 Carfrae Rd. **H17**
6 Cargil Cr. **L19**
6 Cargil Terr. **L19**
3 Cargilfield Sch. **F18**
21 Carlton Cricket Grd. **M14**
2 Carlton Highland Hotel **M16**
1 Carlton St. **L17**
2 Carlton Terr. **N17**
2 Carlton Terr. La. **N17**
2 Carlton Terr. Mews **N17**
14 Carlyle Pl. **O17**
2 Carnegie Ct. **N16**
26 Carnethy Av. **H11**
10 Caroline Gdns. **G16**
5 Caroline Park Av. **J20**
5 Caroline Park Gro. **J19**
9 Caroline Terr. **F16**
Carpet La.* = Bernard St.
18 Carrick Knowe Av. **G15**
18 Carrick Knowe Dr. **G15**
18 Carrick Knowe Gdns. **G15**
18 Carrick Knowe Golf Course **H15**
18 Carrick Knowe Gro. **G15**
18 Carrick Knowe Hill **G15**
18 Carrick Knowe Loan **G15**
18 Carrick Knowe Parkway **G15**
18 Carrick Knowe Pl. **G15**
18 Carrick Knowe Rd. **G14**
18 Carrick Knowe Sch. **G15**
18 Carrick Knowe Terr. **G15**
12 Carrington Rd. **K17**
Carrubber's Cl.* = High St.
7 Casselbank St. **N18**
7 Cassel's La. **N18**

1 Castle **M16**
18 Castle Av. **F15**
1 Castle Esplanade **M16**
1 Castle St. **L16**
1 Castle Terr. **L16**
1 Castle Wynd N. **M16**
1 Castle Wynd S. **M16**
23 Castlebrae Sch. **Q14**
23 Castlebrae Sch. Annexe **Q14**
1 Castlehill **M16**
26 Castlelaw Rd. **H11**
30 Castleview House **P12**
8 Cat & Dog Home **Q18**
12 Cathcart Pl. **K15**
2 Cathedral La. **M17**
19 Cattle Rd. **H14**
14 Causeway, The **P15**
22 Causewayside **N15**
26 Cedars, The **H12**
2 Central Library **M16**
Chalmers Bdgs.* = Fountainbridge
Chalmer's Cl.* = High St.
21 Chalmer's Cr. **M15**
13 Chalmers Hosp. **M16**
13 Chalmer's St. **M15**
20 Chamberlain Rd. **L14**
2 Chambers St. **M16**
7 Chancelot Cr. **M19**
6 Chancelot Gro. **M19**
7 Chancelot Mills **N20**
7 Chancelot Terr. **M19**
23 Chapel Ct. **Q14**
Chapel La.* = Maritime St.
2 Chapel St **N15**
Chapel Wynd* = West Port
2 Charles St. **M16**
2 Charles St. La. **M16**
13 Charlotte St. La. **M16**
1 Charlotte La. **L16**
1 Charlotte Sq. **L16**
21 Charterhall Gro. **M14**
21 Charterhall Rd. **M13**
19 Chesser Av. **H14**
Chesser Cotts.* = Gorgie Rd.
19 Chesser Cr. **J14**
19 Chesser Gdns. **H14**
19 Chesser Gro. **H14**
19 Chesser Ho. **H14**
19 Chesser Loan **H14**
1 Chester St. **L16**
12 Cheyne St. **L17**
11 Choir Sch. **L16**
16 Christian Cr. **R16**
16 Christian Gro. **R16**
15 Christian Path **R16**
15 Christiemiller Av. **Q17**
15 Christiemiller Gro. **Q17**
15 Christiemiller Pl. **Q17**
20 Church Hill **L14**
20 Church Hill Pl. **L14**
20 Church Hill Theatre **L14**
31 Circle, The **R12**
1 Circus Gdns. **L17**
1 Circus La. **L17**
Citadel * = **N19**
7 Citadel St. **N19**
2 City Art Centre **M16**
2 City Chambers **M16**
19 City Hosp. **K12**
2 City Observatory **N17**
26 City of Edinburgh By Pass **G11**
4 Civil Service Sports Ground **H19**
29 Clackmae Gro. **N12**
29 Clackmae Rd. **N12**
22 Clapper La. **O13**
Clapperton Pl.* = Lr. London Rd.
1 Clarebank Cr. **O18**
6 Clarebank St. **M17**
7 Claremont Bank **M17**
7 Claremont Cr. **M18**
8 Claremont Gdns. **O18**
7 Claremont Gro. **M18**

8 Claremont Park **O18**
8 Claremont Rd. **O18**
12 Clarence St. **L17**
1 Clarendon Cr. **L17**
1 Clarendon Hotel **L16**
22 Clarinda Terr. **O13**
6 Clark Av. **M19**
6 Clark Pl. **L19**
6 Clark Rd. **L19**
13 Classic Cinema **N16**
22 Claverhouse Dr. **O12**
22 Clearburn Cr. **O14**
22 Clearburn Gdns. **O14**
22 Clearburn Rd. **O14**
23 Cleekim Dr. **R14**
23 Cleekim Rd. **R14**
24 Cleikiminfield **R14**
24 Cleikiminrig **R14**
13 Clerk St. **N15**
3 Clermiston Av. **F17**
10 Clermiston Cr. **F17**
9 Clermiston Dr. **F17**
9 Clermiston Gdns. **F17**
9 Clermiston Gr. **F17**
10 Clermiston Gro. **F17**
10 Clermiston Hill **F17**
9 Clermiston Loan **F17**
10 Clermiston Medway **F17**
9 Clermiston Park (st.) **F17**
9 Clermiston Park **F17**
10 Clermiston Pl. **F17**
10 Clermiston Rd. **F16**
10 Clermiston Road N. **G17**
9 Clermiston Sch. **F17**
10 Clermiston Terr. **G16**
10 Clermiston View **G17**
9 Clerwood Bank **F16**
9 Clerwood Gdns. **F16**
10 Clerwood Gro. **G16**
9 Clerwood Loan **F16**
10 Clerwood Park **F16**
10 Clerwood Pl. **G16**
9 Clerwood Row **F16**
10 Clerwood Terr. **G16**
10 Clerwood View **G16**
9 Clerwood Way **F16**
Clifton Sq.* = Baileyfield Rd.
12 Clifton Terr. **L16**
20 Clinton Rd. **L14**
14 Clockmill La. **O17**
26 Clovenstone Dr. **G12**
26 Clovenstone Gdns. **G12**
26 Clovenstone Pk. **G12**
26 Clovenstone Rd. **G12**
26 Clovenstone Sch. **G12**
20 Cluny Av. **L13**
20 Cluny Dr. **L13**
21 Cluny Gdns. **L13**
21 Cluny Pl. **M14**
21 Cluny Terr. **L13**
2 Clyde St. **M17**
7 Coalhill **N19**
1 Coates Cr. **L16**
12 Coates Gdns. **K16**
1 Coates Pl. **L16**
7 Coatfield La. **O19**
17 Cobbinshaw House **F13**
21 Cobden Cr. **N14**
20 Cobden Rd. **N14**
1 Cobden Terr. **L16**
7 Coburg St. **N19**
Cochran Pl.* = East London St.
13 Cochran Terr. **M17**
8 Cochrane Pl. **O18**
2 Cockburn St. **M16**
27 Cockit Hat Plantation **K11**
2 Coffin La. **K15**
16 Coillesdene Av. **S16**
16 Coillesdene Cr. **S16**
16 Coillesdene Cr. **S16**
16 Coillesdene Dr. **S16**
16 Coillesdene Gdns. **S16**
16 Coillesdene Gro. **S16**
16 Coillesdene Loan **S16**
16 Coillesdene Terr. **S16**
26 Colinton Castle **H12**

35

26 Colinton Dell H12
19 Colinton Gro. J13
19 Colinton Grove W. J13
27 Colinton Mains Cr. K11
27 Colinton Mains Dr. J12
27 Colinton Mains Gdns. J12
27 Colinton Mains Gr. J12
27 Colinton Mains Gro. K12
27 Colinton Mains Loan J12
27 Colinton Mains Park K12
27 Colinton Mains Pl. K12
27 Colinton Mains Rd. J12
27 Colinton Mains Terr. K12
19 Colinton Rd. H12
27 Colinton Sch. (Primary) J12
12 Colville Pl. L17
21 College of Agriculture N13
1 College of Art M16
17 College of Commerce F13
10 College of Domestic Science F16
2 College St., S. M16
2 College St., W. M16
College Wynd* = Cowgate
2 Collins Pl. L17
11 Coltbridge Av. J16
11 Coltbridge Gdns. K16
11 Coltbridge Terr. J16
11 Coltbridge Vale K16
11 Columba Av. H17
11 Columba Rd. H17
11 Columcille Sch. R16
12 Comely Bank K17
12 Comely Bank Av. L17
11 Comely Bank Cem. K17
12 Comely Bank Gro. K17
12 Comely Bank Pl. L17
12 Comely Bk. Pl. Mews L17
12 Comely Bank Rd. K17
12 Comely Bank Row L17
12 Comely Bank St. K17
12 Comely Bank Terr. L17
14 Comely Gr. Cr. O17
14 Comely Gr. Pl. O17
20 Comiston Dr. K13
20 Comiston Gdns. L13
28 Comiston Gro. L12
20 Comiston Pl. L13
28 Comiston Rise L12
20 Comiston Rd. L12
27 Comiston Sch. K11
28 Comiston Springs Av. L12
20 Comiston Terr. L13
28 Comiston View L12
7 Commercial St. N19
3 Connaught Pl. M19
14 Considine Gdns. P17
14 Considine Terr. P17
7 Constitution Pl. O19
7 Constitution St. O19
Convening Ct.* = Dean Path
4 Corbiehill Av. H18
4 Corbiehill Cr. G18
8 Corbiehill Gdns. H18
4 Corbiehill Gro. H18
4 Corbiehill Pl. G18
4 Corbiehill Rd. G18
4 Corbiehill Terr. G18
24 Corbieshot R15
19 Corn Exchange J14
8 Cornhill Terr. O18
12 Cornwall St. L16
7 Cornwallis Pl. M17
1 Coronation Walk M15
Corporation Bdgs.* = Sheriff Brae
20 Corrennie Dr. L13
25 Corrennie Gdns. L13
25 Corslet Cr. E11
25 Corslet Pl. E11
25 Corslet Rd. E11

9 Corstorphine Bank Av. F16
9 Corstorphine Bank Cotts. F16
9 Corstorphine Bank Dr. F16
9 Corstorphine Bank Terr. F16
9 Corstorphine High St. F15
10 Corstorphine Hill G17
10 Corstorphine Hill Av. G16
9 Corstorphine Hill Cem. F16
10 Corstorphine Hill Cr. G16
10 Corstorphine Hill Gdns. G16
10 Corstorphine Hill Rd. G16
10 Corstorphine Hosp. G15
10 Corstorphine Ho. Av. G15
10 Corstorphine Ho. Terr. G15
10 Corstorphine Park G15
10 Corstorphine Park Gdns. G15
10 Corstorphine Rd. G15
9 Corstorphine Sch. F15
2 Corunna Pl. N19
10 Cottage Park H17
7 County Hall M16
7 Couper St. N19
19 Cowan Rd. K14
2 Cowan's Cl. N15
2 Cowgate M16
2 Cowgatehead M16
10 Craigcrook Av. G17
11 Craigcrook Gdns. Pl. H17
11 Craigcrook Gro. H17
10 Craigcrook Park H17
11 Craigcrook Pl. H17
10 Craigcrook Rd. G18
10 Craigcrook Sq. H17
11 Craigcrook Terr. H17
15 Craigentinny Av. Q17
8 Craigentinny Av. N. P18
15 Craigentinny Cr. Q17
8 Craigentinny Golf Course P18
15 Craigentinny Gro. Q17
15 Craigentinny Pl. Q17
15 Craigentinny Rd. P17
15 Craigentinny Sch. P17
6 Craighall Av. M19
6 Craighall Bank M19
6 Craighall Cr. M19
6 Craighall Gdns. M19
6 Craighall Rd. M19
6 Craighall Terr. M19
20 Craighill Gdns. K13
20 Craighouse Av. K13
20 Craighouse Ct. K13
20 Craighouse Gdns. K13
20 Craighouse Park K13
20 Craighouse Rd. K13
20 Craighouse Terr. K13
9 Craigievar Sq. E16
9 Craigievar Wynd E16
20 Craiglea Dr. K13
20 Craiglea Pl. K13
11 Craigleith Av. N. J16
11 Craigleith Av. S. J16
11 Craigleith Bank J17
11 Craigleith Cr. J17
11 Craigleith Dr. J17
11 Craigleith Gdns. J17
11 Craigleith Gro. J17
11 Craigleith Hill J17
11 Craigleith Hill Av. J17
11 Craigleith Hill Cr. J17
11 Craigleith Hill Gdns. J17
11 Craigleith Hill Gr. J17
11 Craigleith Hill Gro. J17
11 Craigleith Hill Loan J17
11 Craigleith Hill Park J17
11 Craigleith Hill Row J17
11 Craigleith Rise J16
11 Craigleith Rd. J17
11 Craigleith View J16
19 Craiglockhart Av. J13

19 Craiglockhart Bank J13
19 Craiglockhart Cr. J13
19 Craiglockhart Dell J13
19 Craiglockhart Dell Rd. J13
19 Craiglockhart Dr. N. J13
19 Craiglockhart Dr. S. J13
19 Craiglockhart Gdns. J13
19 Craiglockhart Golf Course K13
19 Craiglockhart Gro. J12
19 Craiglockhart Loan J13
19 Craiglockhart Park J13
19 Craiglockhart Pl. J13
19 Craiglockhart Qt. J13
19 Craiglockhart Rd. J13
19 Craiglockhart Rd. N. J13
20 Craiglockhart Sch. K14
19 Craiglockhart Sports Centre J13
19 Craiglockhart Terr. K14
21 Craiglockhart View J13
23 Craigmillar Castle P13
23 Craigmillar Castle Av. P14
23 Craigmillar Castle Gdns. P14
23 Craigmillar Castle Gro. P14
23 Craigmillar Castle Loan Q14
23 Craigmillar Castle Rd. P14
23 Craigmillar Castle Terr. P14
22 Craigmillar House P14
22 Craigmillar Park (street) N14
23 Craigmillar Park P14
21 Craigmillar Park Golf Course N13
23 Craigmillar Sch. Q14
9 Craigmount Appr. F16
9 Craigmount Av. F16
9 Craigmount Av. N. E17
9 Craigmount Bank E17
9 Craigmount Bank W. E17
9 Craigmount Brae E17
9 Craigmount Cr. E16
9 Craigmount Ct. E17
9 Craigmount Dr. E16
9 Craigmount Gdns. E16
9 Craigmount Gro. E16
9 Craigmount Gro. N. E16
9 Craigmount Hill E17
9 Craigmount Loan E16
9 Craigmount Park E16
9 Craigmount Pl. E16
9 Craigmount Sch. E16
9 Craigmount Terr. E16
9 Craigmount View E16
9 Craigmount Way F17
5 Craigmuir Sch. J19
30 Craigour Av. Q12
30 Craigour Cr. Q12
30 Craigour Dr. Q12
30 Craigour Gdns. Q12
30 Craigour Gr. P12
30 Craigour Gro. Q12
30 Craigour Loan Q12
30 Craigour Pl. P12
30 Craigour Terr. Q12
5 Craigroyston Sch. J18
5 Craigs Av. E15
9 Craigs Bank E16
5 Craigs Cr. E16
9 Craigs Dr. E16
9 Craigs Gdns. E16
9 Craigs Gro. F15
9 Craigs Loan F15
9 Craigs Park E16
9 Craigs Rd. E16
3 Cramond Av. E19
3 Cramond Bank E19
3 Cramond Cr. E19
3 Cramond Gdns. E19
3 Cramond Glebe Gdns. F19
3 Cramond Glebe Rd. E19

3 Cramond Glebe Terr. E19
3 Cramond Gr. E19
3 Cramond Gro. E19
3 Cramond Park E19
3 Cramond Park E19
3 Cramond Pl. F19
3 Cramond Regis E18
4 Cramond Rd. N. F19
3 Cramond Rd. S. F19
3 Cramond Sch. E19
3 Cramond Sch. Annexe E19
3 Cramond Terr. E19
3 Cramond Tower F19
3 Cramond Vale E19
2 Cranston St. N16
11 Crarae Av. J16
22 Crawfurd Rd. O14
20 Crescent, The L13
5 Crewe Bank K19
5 Crewe Cr. J19
5 Crewe Gro. K19
5 Crewe Loan J19
5 Crewe Path J19
5 Crewe Pl. J19
5 Crewe Rd. Gdns. J19
5 Crewe Rd. N. J19
5 Crewe Rd. S. K18
5 Crewe Rd. W. J19
5 Crewe Terr. J19
5 Crewe Toll J18
2 Crichton St. M16
7 Crighton Pl. N18
13 Croall Pl. N17
14 Croft-an-righ N17
4 Crown Office Bldgs. N17
17 Cultins Rd. E14
12 Cumberland St. M17
12 Cumberland St. La., N.E. M17
12 Cumberland St. La., N.W. M17
12 Cumberland St. La., S.E. M17
12 Cumberland St. La., S.W. M17
21 Cumin Pl. N15
11 Cumlodden Av. J16
22 Cumnor Cr. O13
7 Cunningham Pl. N18
25 Curriehill Road D11
25 Curriehill Sch. E10
7 Custom House O19

Dairsie Pl.* = Stanley Pl.
Daisy Terr.* = Merchiston Gro.
14 Dalgety Av. O17
14 Dalgety Rd. O17
14 Dalgety St. O17
20 Dalhousie Terr. L13
21 Dalkeith Rd. N15
16 Dalkeith St. S16
7 Dalmeny Park N18
7 Dalmeny Rd. M19
7 Dalmeny St. N18
7 Dalry Cem. K15
12 Dalry Pl. L16
12 Dalry Rd. K15
Dalry Rd. La.* = Dalry Rd.
12 Dalry Sch. K15
21 Dalrymple Cr. N14
Dalziel Pl.* = London Rd.
12 Damside L16
31 Danderhall Cr. R12
31 Danderhall Sch. R12
12 Danube St. L17
12 Darnaway St. L17
7 Darnell Rd. L19
2 David Hume Tower M15
5 Davidson Gdns. H18
5 Davidson Park K18
5 Davidson Rd. J18
4 Davidson's Mains Park G18

4 Davidson's Mains Sch. G18
13 Davie St. N16
13 Deaconess Hosp. N16
13 Dean Bank La. L17
12 Dean Bridge L17
12 Dean Cem. K17
12 Dean Centre K16
14 Dean Cl. P17
12 Dean Park Cr. L17
12 Dean Park Mews L17
12 Dean Park St. L17
12 Dean Path K17
Dean Path Bdgs.* = Dean Path
12 Dean St. L17
12 Dean Terr. L17
12 Deanhaugh St. L17
9 Dechmont Rd. E16
26 Dell Rd. H12
6 Denham Green Av. L19
6 Denham Green Pl. L19
6 Denham Green Terr. L19
9 Derby St. M19
12 Devon Pl. K16
12 Dewar Pl. L16
12 Dewar Pl. La. L16
21 Dick Pl. M14
7 Dickson St. N18
Dickson's Cl.* = High St.
Dickson's Ct.* = Bristo St.
22 Dinmont Dr. O13
Distillery La.* = Dalry Rd.
9 Dochart Dr. F17
7 Dock Pl. N19
7 Dock St. N19
29 Doctor Guthrie's (Boys) Q12
29 Doctor Guthrie's (Girls) Q11
25 Dolphin Gdns. E. D10
20 Dominion Cinema L14
12 Donaldson's Sch. (for the deaf) K16
12 Dorset Pl. L15
22 Double Hedges Pk. O13
22 Double Hedges Rd. O13
12 Douglas Cr. K16
12 Douglas Gdns. K16
12 Douglas Gdns. Mews K16
12 Douglas Terr. L16
12 Doune Terr. L17
18 Dovecot Gro. H13
18 Dovecot Loan H13
18 Dovecot Park H13
18 Dovecot Rd. F15
12 Downfield Pl. K15
10 Downie Gro. G15
10 Downie Terr. G15
12 Dragonara Hotel K16
27 Dreghorn Av. K11
27 Dreghorn Dr. K11
27 Dreghorn Gdns. K11
27 Dreghorn Gro. K11
26 Dreghorn Loan H11
27 Dreghorn Park J11
27 Dreghorn Pl. K11
30 Drum Av. Q11
9 Drum Brae Av. F16
9 Drum Brae Cr. F17
9 Drum Brae Dr. F17
9 Drum Brae Gdns. F16
9 Drum Brae Gro. F17
9 Drum Brae Neuk F16
9 Drum Brae N. E17
9 Drum Brae Park (st.) F16
9 Drum Brae Park F17
Drum Brae Park Appr.* = Drum Brae Pk.
9 Drum Brae Pl. F16
9 Drum Brae S. F16
9 Drum Brae Terr. F17
9 Drum Brae Walk F17
30 Drum Cotts. Q11
30 Drum Cr. Q11

Drum Park Yard* = Albion Rd.
30 Drum Pl. Q11
30 Drum St. Q11
14 Drum Terr. O17
31 Drum View Av. R12
9 Drumbrae Sch. F16
† Drumdryan St. M15
1 Drummond Pl. M17
13 Drummond Sch. M17
27 Drummond Scrolls J11
27 Drummond Scrolls J11
2 Drummond St. N16
1 Drumsheugh Gdns. L16
Drumsheugh Pl* = Queensferry St.
7 Dryden Gdns. N18
21 Dryden Pl. N15
7 Dryden St. N18
7 Dryden Terr. N18
11 Drylaw Av. J17
11 Drylaw Cr. H17
11 Drylaw Gdns. H18
11 Drylaw Gr. H17
11 Drylaw Gro. H17
5 Drylaw Ho. H18
5 Drylaw Ho. Gdns. H18
5 Drylaw Ho. Padd. H18
7 Duart Cr. F17
1 Dublin Meuse M17
2 Dublin St. M17
2 Dublin St. La., N. M17
2 Dublin St. La., S. M17
15 Duddingston Av. Q15
16 Duddingston Cr. R15
15 Duddingston Gdns. N. Q16
15 Duddingston Gdns. S. Q15
15 Duddingston Golf Course Q15
15 Duddingston Gro. E. Q16
15 Duddingston Gro. W. Q15
15 Duddingston Loan Q15
Duddingston Mains Cotts.* = Milton Rd.
15 Duddingston Mills Cotts. Q16
15 Duddingston Park R16
15 Duddingston Park S. R15
15 Duddingston Rise Q15
15 Duddingston Rd. Q16
15 Duddingston Rd. W. P15
15 Duddingston Row Q15
15 Duddingston Sch. Q16
15 Duddingston Sq. E. Q16
15 Duddingston Sq. W. Q16
15 Duddingston Vw. Q15
14 Duddingston Village P15
7 Dudley Av. M19
7 Dudley Av. S. N19
7 Dudley Bank M19
7 Dudley Cr. M19
7 Dudley Gdns. M19
7 Dudley Gro. M19
7 Dudley Terr. M19
12 Duff St. K15
12 Duff St. La. K15
7 Duke Pl. O18
7 Duke St. O18
14 Duke's Walk O17
2 Dumbiedykes Rd. N16
18 Dumbryden Dr. G13
18 Dumbryden Gdns. G13
18 Dumbryden Gro. G13
18 Dumbryden Road G13
18 Dumbryden Sch. G13
1 Dunbar St. L15
1 Duncan Pl. O18
21 Duncan St. N14
13 Dundas St. M17
3 Dundee St. K15
12 Dundee Terr. K15
13 Dundonald St. M17
22 Dundrennan Cotts. P13
9 Dunedin St. M18
3 Dunfermline Coll. of Physical Education F19
Dunlop's Ct.* = Grassmarket

12 Dunrobin Pl. L17
9 Dunsmuir Ct. F15
17 Dunsyre House F13
3 Dunvegan Ct. E18
9 Durar Dr. F17
15 Durham Av. Q16
15 Durham Dr. R15
15 Durham Gdns. N. R16
15 Durham Gdns. S. R15
15 Durham Gro. R16
15 Durham Pl. E. R16
15 Durham Pl. W. Q16
15 Durham Pl. La. R16
15 Durham Rd. R16
15 Durham Rd. S. R15
15 Durham Sq. R16
15 Durham Terr. Q16
22 Durward Gro. O13

1 Earl Grey St. L16
6 Earl Haig Gdns. L19
18 Earl Haig Homes H14
14 Earlston Pl. O17
2 East Adam St. N16
15 East Brighton Cr. R16
28 East Caiystane Pl. L11
28 East Caiystane Rd. L11
20 East Castle Rd. L15
21 East Champanyie N14
22 East Clapperfield O13
7 East Claremont St. M17
11 East Ct. J17
9 East Craigs E16
5 East Craigs Sch. E16
7 East Cromwell St. N19
2 East Crosscauseway N15
6 East Fettes Av. K18
1 East Fountainbridge L16
8 East Hermitage Pl. O18
13 East London St. M17
2 East Market St. N16
21 East Mayfield N14
21 East Newington Pl. N15
13 East Norton Pl. N17
5 East Pilton Park K19
13 East Preston St. N15
2 East Princes St. Gdns. M16
6 East Restalrig Terr. O18
21 East Savile Road N14
13 East Silvermills La. L17
22 East Suffolk Rd. O14
6 East Trinity Rd. L19
East Way, The* = Northfield Cr.
11 Easter Belmont Rd. H16
19 Easter Craiglockhart Hill K13
25 Easter Currie Cr. E11
25 Easter Currie Pl. E11
25 Easter Currie Terr. E10
5 Easter Drylaw Av. J18
5 Easter Drylaw Bank J18
5 Easter Drylaw Dr. J18
5 Easter Drylaw Gdns. J18
5 Easter Drylaw Gro. J18
5 Easter Drylaw Loan J18
5 Easter Drylaw Pl. J18
5 Easter Drylaw View J18
5 Easter Drylaw Way J18
27 Easter Haugh K12
4 Easter Park Dr. G18
14 Easter Rd. N17
4 Eastern Cem. N17
8 Eastern General Hosp. P18
16 Eastfield T16
16 Eastfield Gdns. T16
16 Eastfield Pl. T16
20 Eden La. L14
Eden Pl.* = Newbattle Terr.
14 Edina Pl. O17
13 Edina St. N17
12 Edinburgh Acad. L17
6 Edinburgh Acad. New Field K18

12 Edinburgh Acad. Sports Ground L17
30 Edinburgh Southern Harriers Q12
19 Edinburgh University Sports Ground K14
22 Edinburgh University Sports Gdn. O14
31 Edmonston Dr. R12
31 Edmonstone Rd. R12
31 Edmonstone Terr. R12
19 Education Committee Athletic Grd. J14
12 Eglinton Cr. K16
12 Eglinton St. K16
6 Eildon St. M18
6 Eildon Terr. L18
7 Elbe St. O19
16 Elcho Terr. S16
2 Elder St. M17
15 Electra Pl. R17
12 Elgin Pl. K16
13 Elgin St. S. N17
13 Elgin Terr. N17
22 Ellangowan Terr. P13
30 Ellen's Glen P12
30 Ellen's Glen Rd. P12
11 Ellersly Rd. H16
27 Elliot Gdns. J12
27 Elliot Park J12
27 Elliot Pl. J12
27 Elliot Rd. J12
7 Elliot St. N17
8 Elm Pl. O18
13 Elm Row N17
8 Elmwood Terr. O18
14 Elsie Inglis Memorial Maternity Hosp. O17
19 Eltringham Gdns. J14
19 Eltringham Gro. J14
19 Eltringham Terr. J14
12 Episcopal Theological Coll. K16
Erskine Pl.* = Shandwick Pl.
21 Esdaile M14
3 Esplanade F20
16 Essendale Terr. S16
9 Essendean Pl. F17
9 Essendean Terr. F17
9 Essex Brae E18
3 Essex Park E18
9 Essex Rd. E18
21 Esslemont Rd. N13
11 Esso Motor Hotel J17
20 Ethel Terr. L13
12 Eton Terr. L17
12 Ettrick Gro. L15
20 Ettrick Rd. K14
12 Ettrickdale Pl. L17
21 Eva Pl. N13
12 Eyre Cr. M17
12 Eyre Pl. M17
12 Eyre Terr. M17

3 Fair-a-far Cotts. E19
22 Fairford Gdns. O13
28 Fairmile Av. L11
28 Fairmile Nursing Home M11
28 Fairmilehead L11
28 Fairmilehead Park L11
30 Fala Ct. O11
20 Falcon Av. L14
20 Falcon Ct. L14
20 Falcon Gdns. L14
20 Falcon Rd. L14
20 Falcon Rd. W. L14
10 Falkland Gdns. G17
15 Farrer Gro. Q17
15 Farrer Terr. Q17
9 Fauldburn E17
9 Featherhall Av. F15
9 Featherhall Cr. N. F15
9 Featherhall Cr. S. F15
9 Featherhall Gro. F15

9 Featherhall Pl. **F15**
9 Featherhall Rd. **F15**
9 Featherhall Terr. **F15**
30 Ferniehill Av. **Q11**
30 Ferniehill Dr. **Q11**
30 Ferniehill Gdns. **Q12**
30 Ferniehill Gro. **Q12**
30 Ferniehill Pl. **Q11**
30 Ferniehill Rd. **Q11**
30 Ferniehill Sq. **Q11**
30 Ferniehill St. **Q12**
30 Ferniehill Terr. **Q11**
30 Ferniehill Way **Q12**
26 Fernielaw Av. **H11**
26 Fernielaw Gdns. **H11**
30 Fernieside Av. **Q12**
30 Fernieside Cr. **Q12**
30 Fernieside Dr. **Q12**
30 Fernieside Gdns. **Q12**
30 Fernieside Gro. **Q12**
30 Fernieside Sch. **Q12**
5 Ferry Rd. **H18**
5 Ferry Rd. Av. **J18**
5 Ferry Rd. Dr. **J19**
5 Ferry Rd. Gdns. **J18**
5 Ferry Rd. Gro. **J18**
5 Ferry Rd. Pl. **J18**
6 Ferryfield **L19**
5 Ferryhill Sch. **J18**
2 Festival Fringe Office **M16**
2 Festival Office **M16**
1 Festival Square **L16**
12 Fettes Av. **K17**
6 Fettes Coll. **K18**
6 Fettes Rise **K18**
13 Fettes Row **M17**
4 Fidra Ct. **H19**
16 Figgate Bank **R17**
16 Figgate Burn Park **Q16**
15 Figgate La. **R17**
15 Figgate St. **R17**
15 Fillyside Av. **Q17**
15 Fillyside Rd. **Q18**
15 Fillyside Terr. **Q18**
1 Filmhouse **L16**
21 Findhorn Pl. **N14**
8 Findlay Av. **P18**
8 Findlay Cotts. **P18**
8 Findlay Gdns. **P18**
8 Findlay Gro. **P18**
8 Findlay Medway **P18**
21 Fingal Pl. **M15**
8 Fingzies Pl. **O i8**
27 Firrhill Cr. **K12**
27 Firrhill Dr. **K12**
27 Firrhill Loan **K12**
27 Firrhill Sch. **J12**
7 Fish Market **M20**
7 Fishmarket Sq. **M20**
15 Fishwives' Causeway **Q17**
Fleshmarket Cl.* = High St.
12 Flora Stevenson Sch. **K17**
20 Forbes Rd. **L15**
19 Fords Rd. **H14**
10 Forestry Commission **G15**
5 Forres St. **L17**
13 Forrest Hill **M16**
13 Forrest Rd. **M16**
18 Forrester Park Av. **F14**
18 Forrester Park Dr. **F14**
17 Forrester Park Gdns. **F14**
18 Forrester Park Gr. **G14**
18 Forrester Park Gro. **F14**
18 Forrester Park Loan **F14**
9 Forrester Rd. **F16**
17 Forrester Sch. **F14**
18 Forrester Sch. Annexe **H14**
7 Fort House **N19**
7 Fort Pl. **N19**
7 Fort Sch. **N19**
30 Forteviot House **P12**
2 Forth St. **M17**
25 Forth View Av.**D10**
25 Forth View Cr.(Currie) **D10**
31 Forth View Cr. (Danderhall) **R12**

25 Forth View Rd. **D10**
11 Forthview Rd. **J17**
11 Forthview Terr. **H17**
26 Foulis Cr. **F11**
1 Fountainbridge **L15**
12 Fountainhall Rd. **N14**
20 Fowler Terr. **K15**
10 Fox Covert Av. **G17**
10 Fox Covert Gro. **G17**
10 Fox Covert Sch. **G16**
28 Fox Spring Cr. **L12**
28 Fox Spring Rise **L12**
8 Fox St. **O19**
6 Fraser Av. **L19**
6 Fraser Ct. **L19**
6 Fraser Gdns. **L19**
6 Fraser Gro. **L19**
Fraser Homes* = Spylaw Bank Rd.
1 Frederick St. **M17**
13 Free Church Coll. **M16**
1 Freemasons' Hall **M16**
28 Frogston Av. **L11**
28 Frogston Gdns. **L11**
28 Frogston Gro. **M11**
29 Frogston Rd. E. **N10**
28 Frogston Rd. W. **L11**
28 Frogston Terr. **M11**
19 Fruit Market **J14**
2 Fruit Market Gall **M16**

12 Gabriel's Rd. **L17**
Gabriel's Rd.* = W. Register St.
3 Gamekeeper's Loan **E19**
3 Gamekeeper's Pk. **E18**
3 Gamekeeper's Rd. **E19**
4 Garden Terr. **G18**
10 Gardiner Gro. **H17**
10 Gardiner Rd. **H17**
10 Gardiner Terr. **H17**
Gardner St.* = Lower London Rd.
1 Gardner's Cr. **L16**
21 Garscube Terr. **J16**
29 Garvald Ct. **O11**
13 Gayfield Pl. **N17**
13 Gayfield Pl. La. **N17**
13 Gayfield Sq. **N17**
13 Gayfield St. **N17**
2 General Post Office **M16**
General's Entry* = Bristo St.
2 George IV Bridge **M16**
2 George Heriot's Sch.
6 George Heriot's Sports Ground **L15**
1 George Hotel **M17**
5 George Pl. **N18**
2 George Sq. **M15**
2 George Sq. La. **M15**
1 George St. **L16**
20 George Watson's Coll. **L14**
20 George Watson's Coll. Recreation Ground **K14**
Gibb's Entry* = Simon Sq.
5 Gibson St. **N18**
12 Gibson Terr. **L15**
2 Gifford Park **N15**
Gilchrist's Entry* = Leith St.
Gilchrist's La.* = Greenside Row
12 Giles St. **N18**
12 Gillespie Cr. **L15**
12 Gillespie Pl. **L15**
26 Gillespie Rd. **G11**
12 Gillespie St. **L15**
20 Gillsland Rd. **K14**
30 Gilmerton Dykes Av. **P11**

30 Gilmerton Dykes Cr. **P11**
30 Gilmerton Dykes Dr. **P11**
30 Gilmerton Dykes Gdns. **P11**
30 Gilmerton Dykes Gro. **P11**
30 Gilmerton Dykes Loan **P11**
30 Gilmerton Dykes Pl. **P11**
30 Gilmerton Dykes Rd. **P10**
30 Gilmerton Dykes St. **P11**
30 Gilmerton Dykes Terr. **P11**
30 Gilmerton Dykes View **P11**
30 Gilmerton Park **Q12**
22 Gilmerton Rd. **O13**
30 Gilmerton Sch. **P11**
30 Gilmerton Station Rd. **Q11**
12 Gilmore Park **L15**
12 Gilmore Pl. **L15**
12 Gilmore Pl.La. **L15**
21 Gilmour Rd. **N14**
2 Gilmour St. **N16**
6 Gladstone Pl. **O18**
13 Gladstone Terr. **N15**
Glanville Pl.* = Kerr St.
9 Glasgow Rd. **E15**
10 Glebe Gdns. **G15**
10 Glebe Gro. **F15**
10 Glebe Rd. **F15**
10 Glebe Terr. **F15**
1 Glen St. **M15**
22 Glenallan Dr. **O13**
22 Glenallan Loan **O13**
18 Glenalmond Court **F13**
12 Glencairn Cr. **K16**
11 Glendevon Av. **H15**
11 Glendevon Gdns. **H15**
11 Glendevon Gro. **H15**
11 Glendevon Park **H15**
11 Glendevon Pl. **H15**
11 Glendevon Rd. **H15**
11 Glendevon Terr. **H15**
29 Glendinning Cr. **O12**
1 Glenfinlas St. **L16**
1 Glengyle Terr. **L15**
21 Glenisla Gdns. **M14**
Glenisla Gdns. La* = Glenisla Gdns.
14 Glenlee Av. **P16**
14 Glenlee Gdns. **P16**
13 Glenlockhart Bank **J13**
19 Glenlockhart Rd. **J13**
19 Glenlockhart Valley **J13**
Glenogle Pl.* = Bell Pl.
12 Glenogle Rd. **L17**
12 Glenogle Terr. **L18**
Glenorchy Pl.* = Greenside Row
21 Glenorchy Terr. **N14**
9 Glenure Loan **F17**
22 Glenvarloch Cr. **O12**
1 Gloucester La. **L17**
1 Gloucester Pl. **L17**
Gloucester Sq.* = Gloucester St.
1 Gloucester St. **L17**
15 Goff Av. **Q17**
17 Gogarloch Rd **E15**
6 Goldenacre Terr. **L18**
10 Gordon Loan **G16**
10 Gordon Rd. **G16**
7 Gordon St. **O18**
22 Gordon Terr. **O13**
Gorgie Cotts.* = Gorgie Rd.
19 Gorgie Rd. **H14**
7 Gosford Pl. **M19**
13 G.P.O. Sorting Office **N17**
22 Gracemount Av. **O12**
29 Gracemount Dr. **O11**
30 Gracemount Park **P11**
29 Gracemount Pl. **O11**

29 Gracemount Rd. **O11**
30 Gracemount Sch. **O11**
30 Gracemount Sch. (Secondary) **P11**
29 Gracemount Sq. **O12**
7 Graham St. **N19**
7 Grampian House **N19**
21 Granby Rd. **N14**
21 Grange Cem. **M14**
Grange Ct.* = Causewayside
21 Grange Cr. **M14**
12 Grange Cricket Grd. **L17**
21 Grange Loan **M14**
21 Grange Loan Gdns. **M14**
21 Grange Rd. **M15**
21 Grange Terr. **M14**
26 Grant Av. **H11**
5 Granton Cr. **K19**
6 Granton Cr. Park **K19**
6 Granton Gdns. **K19**
6 Granton Gro. **K19**
5 Granton Medway **K19**
5 Granton Park Av. **K20**
6 Granton Pl. **K19**
6 Granton Rd. **L19**
5 Granton Sch. **K19**
6 Granton Sq. **K20**
6 Granton Terr. **K19**
6 Granton View **K19**
20 Granville Terr. **L15**
2 Gray's Loan **K14**
19 Graysmill Sch. **H13**
15 Great Canon Bk. **R17**
7 Great Junction St. **N19**
1 Great King St. **M17**
7 Great Michael Rise **M19**
Great Michael Sq.* = Main St.
1 Great Stuart St. **L16**
13 Green St. **M17**
4 Green, The **G18**
26 Green Way, The **G12**
20 Greenbank Av. **L13**
20 Greenbank Cr. **K12**
20 Greenbank Dr. **K13**
20 Greenbank Gdns. **K12**
28 Greenbank Gro. **K12**
20 Greenbank La. **K13**
20 Greenbank Loan **K12**
20 Greenbank Park **K12**
20 Greenbank Pl. **L13**
28 Greenbank Rise **K12**
20 Greenbank Rd. **K12**
28 Greenbank Row. **K12**
20 Greenbank Terr. **L13**
23 Greendykes Av. **Q14**
23 Greendykes Dr. **Q14**
23 Greendykes Gdns. **Q14**
23 Greendykes House **Q14**
23 Greendykes Loan **Q14**
23 Greendykes Rd. **Q14**
23 Greendykes Sch. **Q14**
23 Greendykes Terr. **Q14**
30 Greenend Dr. **P12**
30 Greenend Gdns. **P12**
30 Greenend Gro. **P12**
20 Greenhill Gdns. **L15**
20 Greenhill Park **L14**
20 Greenhill Pl. **L14**
20 Greenhill Terr. **L15**
22 Greenmantle Loan **O12**
12 Green's Hotel **K16**
Greenside Ct.* = Greenside Row
2 Greenside La. **N17**
2 Greenside Pl. **N17**
2 Greenside Row **N17**
13 Greyfriars Kirk **M16**
Greyfriars Pl.* = Candlemaker Row
6 Grierson Av. **L19**
6 Grierson Cr. **L19**
6 Grierson Gdns. **L19**
6 Grierson Rd. **K19**
6 Grierson Sq. **L19**

6 Grierson Villas L19
5 Grigor Av. J18
5 Grigor Dr. J18
5 Grigor Gdns. J19
5 Grigor Terr. J18
1 Grindlay St. L16
11 Groathill Av. J17
11 Groathill Gdns E. J17
11 Groathill Gdns W. J17
5 Groathill Road N. J18
11 Groathill Road S. J17
12 Grosvenor Centre Hotel
   L16
12 Grosvenor Cr. K16
12 Grosvenor Gdns. K16
12 Grosvenor St. L16
25 Grove Pl. F11
12 Grove St. L16
   Grove Terr.* = Grove St.
2 Gullan's Cl. N16
2 Gunnet Ct. H19
2 Guthrie St. M16
9 Gyle Park, The E15
9 Gyle Park Gdns. E15
9 Gylemuir Rd. F15
9 Gylemuir Sch. F15
5 Gypsy Brae H20

13 Haddington Pl. N17
   Haddington's Entry* =
     Reid's Cl.
   Haddon Ct.* =
     Howden St.
26 Hailes Approach H12
26 Hailes Av. H12
26 Hailes Bank H12
26 Hailes Cr. H12
26 Hailes Gdns. G12
26 Hailes Gro. H12
26 Hailes Park (street)
   G12
18 Hailes Park G13
1 Hailes St. L15
26 Hailes Terr. H12
18 Hailesland Gdns. G13
18 Hailesland Gro. G13
18 Hailesland Park G13
18 Hailesland Pl. G13
18 Hailesland Rd. F13
26 Hailesland Sch. G12
10 Hall Terr. G15
22 Hallhead Rd N13
3 Halmyre St. N18
7 Hamilton Cr. N19
12 Hamilton Dr. Q16
15 Hamilton Dr. W. Q16
15 Hamilton Gdns. Q16
15 Hamilton Gro. Q16
15 Hamilton Park Q16
12 Hamilton Pl. L17
7 Hamilton St. N19
15 Hamilton Terr. R16
7 Hamilton Wynd N19
   Hampton Pl.* =
     West Catherine Pl.
11 Hampton Terr. K16
1 Hanover St. M17
20 Harden Pl. K15
13 Hardwell Cl. N15
26 Harelaw Rd. H11
23 Harewood Cr. Q14
23 Harewood Dr. Q14
23 Harewood Rd. Q14
19 Harrison Gdns. K14
20 Harrison La. K15
20 Harrison Park K15
19 Harrison Pl. K14
20 Harrison Rd. K15
2 Hart St. M17
   Hart St. La.* = Hart St.
20 Hartington Gdns. L15
20 Hartington Pl. L15
21 Hatton Pl. M15
12 Haugh St. L17
29 Hawkhead Cr. O12
29 Hawkhead Gro. O12

7 Hawkhill Av. O18
8 Hawkhill Ct. O18
   Hawkhill Villas* =
     Lochend Rd.
   Hawthorn Bdgs.* =
     Belford Rd.
   Hawthorn Terr.* =
     Hawthornbank La.
12 Hawthornbank La. L16
7 Hawthornbank Pl. M19
7 Hawthornbank Terr. N19
30 Hawthorne Pl. Q11
7 Hawthornvale M19
23 Hay Av. Q14
23 Hay Dr. R14
23 Hay Pl. Q14
23 Hay Rd. Q14
23 Hay Terr. Q14
9 Hayfield E16
1 Haymarket L16
12 Haymarket Sta. L16
12 Haymarket Terr. K16
19 Hazelbank Terr. K14
22 Hazeldean Terr. O13
22 Hazelwood Gro. P13
22 Headrigg Row O13
19 Heart of Midlothian
     Stadium K15
11 Henderland Rd. J16
7 Henderson Gdns. N19
12 Henderson Pl. M17
12 Henderson Row. L17
7 Henderson St. N19
12 Henderson Terr. K15
13 Henry St. N15
13 Heriot Bridge M16
   Heriot Cross* = Heriot Br.
7 Heriot Hill Terr. M18
13 Heriot Pl. M16
12 Heriot Row L17
25 Heriot-Watt University
   &2 D12, M16
19 Hermand Cr. K14
19 Hermand St. J14
19 Hermand Terr. J14
17 Hermiston Court F13
20 Hermitage Dr. L13
20 Hermitage Gdns. L13
20 Hermitage of Braid L13
8 Hermitage Park O18
8 Hermitage Park Sch. O18
8 Hermitage Park S. O18
20 Hermitage Pl. O18
20 Hermitage Terr. L13
7 Hibernian Stadium O17
1 High Riggs L16
13 High School Yards N16
3 High St. M16
15 Highway, The Q16
2 Hill Pl. N16
1 Hill Sq. N16
12 Hill St. L17
12 Hill St. La. N. L17
12 Hill St. La. S. M17
15 Hillcoat Ln. R17
15 Hillcoat Pl. R17
   Hillend Pl.* = London Rd.
28 Hillend Ski Slope L10
4 Hillhouse Rd. G18
10 Hillpark Av. G18
10 Hillpark Brae G17
10 Hillpark Ct. G18
10 Hillpark Cr. G17
10 Hillpark Dr. G18
10 Hillpark Gdns. G17
10 Hillpark Gro. G17
10 Hillpark Loan H17
10 Hillpark Pl. G17
10 Hillpark Rd. G17
10 Hillpark Terr. G17
10 Hillpark View G17
10 Hillpark Way H17
10 Hillpark Wood H17
13 Hillside Cr. N17
13 Hillside St. N17
24 Hilltown Terr. S13
11 Hillview H17
9 Hillview Cr. F16

9 Hillview Dr. F16
9 Hillview Rd. F16
9 Hillview Terr. F16
19 Hollybank Terr. K14
6 Holy Cross Sch. M19
15 Holy Rood Sch. P15
13 Holyrood Ct. N16
14 Holyrood Park O16
13 Holyrood Park Rd. N15
2 Holyrood Rd. N16
2 Holyrood Terr. N15
2 Holyroodhouse, Palace of
   N16
12 Home St. L15
16 Hope La. R16
13 Hope Park Cr. N15
   Hope Park Sq.* =
     Meadow La.
13 Hope Park Terr. N15
12 Hope St. L16
12 Hope St. La. L16
20 Hope Terr. M14
7 Hopefield Terr. N19
13 Hopetoun Cr. N17
13 Hopetoun Cr. La. N17
7 Hopetoun St. N18
12 Horne Terr. L15
13 Horse Wynd N16
9 Hoseason Gdns. F17
24 Hosie Rigg R15
4 House o' Hill Av. H18
4 House o' Hill Brae H18
4 House o' Hill Cr. H18
4 House o' Hill Gdns. H18
4 House o' Hill Gr. H18
4 House o' Hill Gro. H18
4 House o' Hill Pl. H18
4 House o' Hill Rd. H18
4 House o' Hill Row H18
4 House o' Hill Terr. H17
6 Howard Pl. M18
6 Howard St M18
29 Howden Hall Ct. N11
29 Howden Hall Cr. N11
29 Howden Hall Dr. N11
29 Howden Hall Gdns. O11
29 Howden Hall Loan N11
29 Howden Hall Park N11
29 Howden Hall Rd. O11
29 Howden Hall Way O11
2 Howden Pk. N11
2 Howden St. N15
1 Howe St. M17
12 Hugh Miller Pl. L17
2 Hunter Sq. M16
27 Hunter's Tryst K11
27 Hunter's Tryst Sch. K12
6 Huntly St. M18
19 Hutchison Av. J14
19 Hutchison Cotts. J14
19 Hutchison Crossway J14
19 Hutchison Gdns. J14
19 Hutchison Gro. J14
19 Hutchison House J14
19 Hutchison Loan J14
19 Hutchison Medway J14
19 Hutchison Pl. J14
19 Hutchison Rd. J14
19 Hutchison Terr. J14
19 Hutchison View J14
30 Hyvot Av. P11
30 Hyvot Ct. P11
30 Hyvot Dr. P11
30 Hyvot Gdns. P11
30 Hyvot Gr. P11
30 Hyvot Gro. P11
30 Hyvot Loan P11
30 Hyvot Park P11
30 Hyvot Terr. P11
30 Hyvot View P11
30 Hyvot's Bank Av. Q11
30 Hyvot's Bank Valley
     Park P11

11 Ice Rink, Murrayfield J15
22 Inch Park, The O13
5 Inchcolm Ct. J19

5 Inchgarvie Ct. J18
7 Inchkeith Ct. N18
4 Inchmickery Ct. H19
5 Inchview Sch. J18
15 Inchview Terr. Q17
   India Bdgs.* = Victoria St.
12 India Pl. L17
12 India St. L17
8 Industrial Rd. O18
   Industry Home* =
     Industry La.
7 Industry La. N19
2 Infirmary St. N16
29 Inglewood Pl. O12
   Inglis' Ct.* = West Port
19 Inglis Green Rd. H13
3 Inveralmond Dr. E19
3 Inveralmond Gdns. E19
3 Inveralmond Gr. E19
6 Inverleith Av. L18
6 Inverleith Av. S. L18
6 Inverleith Gdns. L18
6 Inverleith Gro. K18
6 Inverleith Ho. L18
6 Inverleith Park L18
6 Inverleith Pl. L18
6 Inverleith Place La. L18
6 Inverleith Row L18
6 Inverleith Terr. L18
6 Inverleith Terr. La. L18
7 Iona St. N18
2 Ivanhoe Cr. O13
19 Ivy Terr. K15

23 Jack Kane Centre R14
1 Jamaica St. L17
1 Jamaica St. N. La. L17
1 Jamaica St. S. La. L17
2 James' Ct.* = Lawnmarket
13 James Craig Walk* =
     Leith St.
21 James Gillespie's
     Sch. M15
21 James Gillespie's Sch.
     Annexe M15
16 James St. S16
16 James St. La. S16
7 Jameson Pl. N18
7 Jane St. N18
   Jane Terr.* =
     Comely Green Cr.
2 Jawbone Walk M15
22 Jean Armour Av. O13
11 Jeffrey Av. H17
2 Jeffrey St. N16
6 Jessfield Terr. M19
23 Jewel Park R15
23 Jewel, The R15
14 Jock's Lodge P17
23 John Russel Ct. N19
16 John St. S16
16 John St. La. S16
7 John's La. O19
7 John's Pl. O19
1 Johnston Terr. M16
16 Joppa Gdns. S16
16 Joppa Gro. S16
16 Joppa Park S16
16 Joppa Quarry Park S16
16 Joppa Rd. S16
16 Joppa Terr. S16
20 Jordan La. L14
2 Junction Pl. N19
25 Juniper Av. F11
25 Juniper Green Sch. F11
25 Juniper Green Sch.
     Annexe F11
25 Juniper Gro. F11
25 Juniper Park Rd. F11
25 Juniper Terr. F11

10 Kaimes Rd. G16
26 Kaimes Sch. P11
31 Kaimes Vw. R12
26 Katesmill Rd. H12
7 Keddie Gdns. N19

29 Kedslie Pl. **N12**
29 Kedslie Rd. **N12**
1 Keir St. **M16**
10 Keith Cr. **H17**
11 Keith Row **J17**
10 Keith Terr. **H17**
15 Kekewich Av. **Q17**
12 Kemp Pl. **L17**
29 Kenilworth Dr. **O12**
14 Kenmure Av. **P16**
1 Kerr St. **L17**
11 Kew Terr. **K16**
21 Kilgraston Ct. **M14**
21 Kilgraston Rd. **M14**
22 Kilmaurs Rd. **O14**
22 Kilmaurs Terr. **O14**
11 Kinellan Rd. **J16**
13 King George V Park **M17**
13 King James Hotel **M17**
7 King St. **N19**
7 Kinghorn Pl. **M19**
1 King's Bridge **N19**
21 King's Bdgs., The **N13**
22 King's Haugh **P14**
15 King's Place **R17**
15 King's Rd. **R17**
1 King's Stables Rd. **L16**
1 King's Stables La. **M16**
15 King's Terr. **Q17**
1 King's Theatre **L15**
11 Kingsburgh Rd. **J16**
22 Kingsinch Sch. **O13**
18 Kingsknowe Av. **H13**
18 Kingsknowe Cr. **H13**
18 Kingsknowe Ct. **G13**
18 Kingsknowe Dr. **H13**
26 Kingsknowe Gdns. **H12**
26 Kingsknowe Golf
    Course **G12**
26 Kingsknowe Gro. **H12**
26 Kingsknowe Park **H12**
18 Kingsknowe Pl. **G13**
18 Kingsknowe Rd. N. **H13**
18 Kingsknowe Rd. S. **H13**
18 Kingsknowe Sta. **H13**
18 Kingsknowe Terr. **H13**
22 Kingston Av. **P13**
6 Kinnear Rd. **K18**
22 Kirkbrae **O13**
10 Kirk Loan **G15**
29 Kirk Park **O12**
7 Kirk St. **N18**
Kirkgate, Leith* =
    Leith Walk
29 Kirkgate, Liberton **O12**
7 Kirkgate Ho. **O19**
22 Kirkhill Dr. **O14**
22 Kirkhill Gdns. **O15**
22 Kirkhill Rd. **O15**
22 Kirkhill Terr. **O15**
Kirkwood Pl.* =
    London Rd.

13 Lady Lawson St. **M16**
14 Lady Menzies Pl. **O17**
15 Lady Nairne Cr., **P16**
15 Lady Nairne Gro. **P16**
15 Lady Nairne Loan **P16**
15 Lady Nairne Pl. **P16**
22 Lady Rd. **O14**
1 Lady Stair's Cl. **M16**
13 Lady Wynd **M16**
21 Ladysmith Rd. **N13**
9 Ladywell Av. **F15**
9 Ladywell Gdns. **F15**
9 Ladywell Ho. **F15**
9 Ladywell Rd. **F15**
19 Laichpark Pl. **J14**
19 Laichpark Rd. **H15**
16 Laing Terr. **S16**
Lamb's Cl.* =
    East Crosscauseway
22 Lamermoor Terr. **P13**
22 Lampacre Rd. **G15**
26 Lanark Rd. **F11**
25 Lanark Rd. W. **D10**

30 Langloan Rd. **P10**
21 Langton Rd. **N14**
12 Lansdowne Cr. **K16**
11 Lapicide Pl. **N19**
7 Largo Pl. **N19**
30 Lasswade Bank **P11**
30 Lasswade Gro. **P11**
22 Lasswade Rd. **O12**
21 Lauder Ln. **N14**
21 Lauder Rd. **M15**
21 Lauderdale St. **M15**
20 Laurel Terr. **K15**
1 Laurie St. **O18**
4 Lauriston Castle **G19**
21 Lauriston Dental Centre
    N14
4 Lauriston Farm Rd. **G18**
13 Lauriston Gdns. **M15**
13 Lauriston Park **M15**
13 Lauriston Pl. **M16**
13 Lauriston St. **M16**
13 Lauriston Terr. **M16**
6 Laverockbank Av. **M19**
6 Laverockbank Cr. **M19**
6 Laverockbank Gdns. **M19**
6 Laverockbank Gro. **M19**
6 Laverockbank Rd. **M19**
6 Laverockbank Terr. **M19**
26 Laverockdale Cr. **H11**
26 Laverockdale Loan **H11**
26 Laverockdale Park **H11**
1 Lawnmarket **M16**
29 Leadervale Rd. **N12**
29 Leadervale Terr. **N12**
Leamington Pl.* =
    Leamington Terr.
12 Leamington Rd. **L15**
20 Leamington Terr. **L15**
12 Learmonth Av. **K17**
12 Learmonth Cr. **K17**
12 Learmonth Ct. **K17**
12 Learmonth Gdns. **K17**
1 Learmonth Gdns. Mews
    L17
12 Learmonth Gro. **K17**
12 Learmonth Hotel **K17**
12 Learmonth Park **K17**
12 Learmonth Pl. **K17**
12 Learmonth Terr. **K17**
12 Learmonth Terr. La. **K17**
2 Lecture Theatre **M16**
15 Lee Cr. **R16**
7 Leith **N19**
7 Leith Acad. **O18**
7 Leith Acad. Annexe **O18**
14 Leith Acad. Annexe **O17**
7 Leith Hosp. **N19**
7 Leith Links **O18**
7 Leith Nautical Coll. **S15**
7 Leith Sch. (Primary) **O18**
13 Leith St. **M17**
13 Leith Walk **N17**
13 Leith Walk Sch. **N17**
11 Lennel Av. **J16**
6 Lennox Row **L19**
12 Lennox St. **L17**
12 Lennox St. La. **L17**
13 Leopold Pl. **N17**
12 Leslie Pl. **L17**
1 Leven St. **L15**
12 Leven Terr. **M15**
12 Lewis Terr. **L16**
22 Liberton Brae **O13**
29 Liberton Cem. **O12**
29 Liberton Dr. **N12**
22 Liberton Gdns. **O11**
22 Liberton Golf Course **P13**
30 Liberton Hosp. **O11**
29 Liberton Park **O12**
30 Liberton Sch. **P12**
22 Liberton Sch. Annexe
    P13
22 Liberton Sch. (Primary)
    O13
12 Liddesdale Pl. **L17**
Lily Terr.* = Shandon Pl.
14 Lilyhill Terr. **P17**
20 Limes, The **L14**

8 Lindean Pl. **O18**
Lindsay Pl.* =
    Chambers St.
7 Lindsay Rd. **N19**
7 Lindsay St. **N19**
8 Links Gdns. **O19**
8 Links Gdns. La. **O19**
8 Links Gro. **O19**
7 Links La. **O19**
7 Links Pl. **O19**
7 Linksview Ho. **O19**
14 Lismore Av. **P17**
14 Lismore Cr. **P17**
15 Lismore Sch. **Q15**
30 Little France Ho. **P12**
1 Little Lyceum **L16**
29 Little Rd. **O12**
7 Livingstone Pl. **M15**
6 Lixmount Av. **M19**
6 Lixmount Gdns. **M19**
14 Loaning Cres. **P17**
14 Loaning Rd. **P17**
10 Loch Rd. **H17**
8 Lochend Av. **O18**
Lochend Cl.* =
    Canongate
14 Lochend Cr. **P17**
14 Lochend Dr. **O17**
14 Lochend Gdns. **O17**
14 Lochend Gro. **P17**
14 Lochend Ho. **P17**
14 Lochend Park (street)
    O17
14 Lochend Park **O17**
14 Lochend Qt. **P17**
7 Lochend Rd. **O18**
14 Lochend Rd. S. **O17**
14 Lochend Sq. **O17**
22 Lochrin Bdgs. **L15**
1 Lochrin La. **L15**
12 Lochrin Pl. **L15**
Lochrin Terr.* =
    Thornybauk
13 Lochview Ct. **N16**
30 Lockerby Cotts. **P11**
30 Lockerby Cr. **P11**
30 Lockerby Gro. **P11**
19 Lockharton Av. **J13**
19 Lockharton Cr. **K13**
19 Lockharton Gdns. **K14**
12 Logan St. **M17**
14 Loganlea Av. **P17**
14 Loganlea Dr. **P17**
14 Loganlea Gdns. **P17**
14 Loganlea Loan **P17**
14 Loganlea Pl. **P17**
14 Loganlea Rd. **P17**
14 Loganlea Terr. **P17**
6 Logie Green Gdns. **M18**
6 Logie Green Loan **M18**
6 Logie Green Rd. **M18**
6 Lomond Rd. **L19**
2 London Rd. **N17**
7 London Row **N19**
13 London St. **M17**
13 London St. Sch. **N17**
29 Longformacus Rd. **O12**
21 Longmore Hosp. **N15**
18 Longstone Av. **H13**
Longstone Cotts.* =
    Longstone Rd.
18 Longstone Cr. **H14**
18 Longstone Gdns. **G14**
18 Longstone Gro. **H13**
18 Longstone Park **H13**
18 Longstone Rd. **G13**
18 Longstone Sch. **H13**
18 Longstone St. **H13**
18 Longstone Terr. **G14**
18 Longstone View **G14**
13 Lonsdale Terr. **M15**
Lord Russell Pl.* =
    Causewayside
7 Lorne Pl. **N18**
7 Lorne Sch. **N18**
7 Lorne Sq. **N18**
7 Lorne St. **N18**
1 Lothian Ho. **L16**

1 Lothian Rd. **L16**
2 Lothian St. **M16**
28 Lothianburn Golf Course
    L10
21 Lovers' Loan **M15**
12 Lower Gilmore Pl. **L15**
6 Lower Granton Rd. **K20**
16 Lower Joppa **S16**
14 Lower London Rd. **O17**
21 Lussielaw Rd. **N13**
13 Lutton Pl. **N15**
12 Lyceum Theatre **L16**
22 Lygon Rd. **N13**
14 Lyne St. **O17**
1 Lynedoch Pl. **L16**
1 Lynedoch Pl. La. **L16**

7 McDonald Pl. **M18**
7 McDonald Rd. **M18**
7 McDonald St. **N18**
21 McDowall Rd. **N14**
2 McEwan Hall **M16**
6 McKelvie Parade **L20**
22 McLaren Rd. **O14**
12 McLaren Terr. **L16**
11 McLeod St. **K15**
12 McNeill St. **L15**
7 Madeira Pl. **N19**
7 Madeira St. **N19**
12 Magdala Cr. **K16**
12 Magdala Mews **K16**
16 Magdalene Av. **R15**
16 Magdalene Ct. **R15**
16 Magdalene Dr. **R15**
16 Magdalene Gdns. **R15**
16 Magdalene Loan **R15**
16 Magdalene Medway **R15**
16 Magdalene Pl. **R15**
11 Maidencraig Cr. **J17**
11 Maidencraig Cr. **J17**
11 Maidencraig Gro. **J17**
13 Main Point **M16**
4 Main St. **G18**
12 Malta Terr. **L17**
Malta Green* =
    St. Bernard's Row
7 Manderston St. **N18**
29 Mannering Pl. **O12**
1 Manor Pl. **L16**
10 Manse Rd. **F15**
9 Manse St. **F15**
13 Mansfield Pl. **M17**
21 Mansionhouse Rd. **M15**
10 March Gro. **G17**
10 March Rd. **G17**
Marchfield Gdns.* =
    Hillhouse Rd.
4 Marchfield Gro. **H18**
4 Marchfield Park **G18**
4 Marchfield Terr. **H17**
22 Marchhall Cr. **O15**
22 Marchhall Pl. **O15**
22 Marchhall Rd. **O15**
21 Marchmont Cr. **M15**
21 Marchmont Rd. **M15**
21 Marchmont St. **M15**
20 Mardale Cr. **L14**
4 Marine Dr. **G19**
8 Marine Esplanade **P19**
15 Marine Gardens Industrial
    Site **Q17**
14 Marionville Av. **O17**
14 Marionville Cr. **P17**
14 Marionville Dr. **P17**
14 Marionville Gro. **P17**
14 Marionville Park **O17**
14 Marionville Rd. **O17**
Marischal Pl.* =
    Queensferry Rd.
7 Maritime La. **O19**
7 Maritime St. **N19**
2 Market St. **M16**
16 Marlborough St. **R16**
22 Marmion Cr. **O13**
Marshall Pl.* =
    Kirkwood Pl.

2 Marshall St. **M16**
2 Marshall's Ct. **N17**
7 Martello Ct. **H19**
Martin's Ct.* =
Bernard St.
11 Mary Erskine Sch. for
Girls, The **H16**
14 Maryfield, Abbeyhill **N17**
15 Maryfield, Portobello **R17**
14 Maryfield Pl. **O17**
Mary's Pl.* = Raeburn Pl.
30 Marytree House **P12**
21 Masson Hall **N14**
31 Maulsford Av. **R12**
21 Maurice Pl. **M13**
20 Maxwell St. **L14**
4 May Ct. **H19**
Maybank Villas* =
St. John's Rd.
9 Maybury Dr. **E16**
9 Maybury Rd. **E17**
21 Mayfield Gdns. **N14**
Mayfield Pl.* = St. John's
Rd.
21 Mayfield Rd. **N14**
21 Mayfield Terr. **N14**
6 Mayville Gdns. E. **M19**
13 Meadow La. **M15**
21 Meadow Pl. **M15**
21 Meadow Pl.La **M15**
17 Meadow Pl. Rd. **F15**
14 Meadowbank Av. **O17**
14 Meadowbank Cr. **O17**
Meadowbank Pl.* =
London Rd.
14 Meadowbank Sports
Centre **O17**
14 Meadowbank Terr. **O17**
15 Meadowfield Av. **P16**
14 Meadowfield Dr. **P16**
14 Meadowfield Gdns. **P15**
14 Meadowfield Terr. **P15**
14 Meadowhead Pk. **P16**
10 Meadowhouse Rd. **G15**
15 Meadowplace Rd. **F15**
13 Meadows, The **M15**
9 Mearnside **E16**
2 Medical School **M16**
17 Medwin House **F13**
19 Meggetland Athletic Grd.
J14
19 Meggetland Terr. **K14**
Melbourne Pl.* =
George IV Bridge
13 Melgund Terr. **M17**
1 Melville Cr. **L16**
1 Melville Dr. **M15**
31 Melville Gate Rd. **S10**
31 Melville Nurseries **S10**
Melville Pl.* =
Queensferry St.
1 Melville St. **L16**
1 Melville St. La. **L16**
21 Melville Terr. **M15**
15 Mentone Av. **R17**
21 Mentone Gdns. **N14**
21 Mentone Terr. **N14**
Merchant St.* =
Candlemaker Row
20 Merchiston Av. **L15**
20 Merchiston Bank Av. **L14**
20 Merchiston Bk. Gdns. **L14**
26 Merchiston Castle Sch.
H12
20 Merchiston Cr. **L14**
20 Merchiston Gdns. **K14**
19 Merchiston Gro. **K14**
20 Merchiston Mews **L15**
20 Merchiston Park **L15**
20 Merchiston Pl. **L15**
20 Mertoun Pl. **K15**
2 Meuse La. **M16**
22 Mid Liberton **O13**
13 Middle Meadow Walk
M15
21 Middleby St. **N14**
7 Middlefield **N18**
21 Midmar Av. **M13**

21 Midmar Dr. **M13**
21 Midmar Gdns. **L13**
7 Mill La. **N19**
20 Millar Cr. **L14**
20 Millar Pl. **L14**
1 Miller Row **L16**
21 Millerfield Pl. **M15**
24 Millerhill Rd. **R13**
15 Milton Cr. **R15**
16 Milton Dr. **S16**
15 Milton Gdns. N. **R15**
15 Milton Gdns. S. **R15**
16 Milton Gro. **T16**
15 Milton Rd. **R15**
16 Milton Rd. E. **S15**
15 Milton Rd. W. **Q15**
14 Milton St. **O17**
16 Milton Terr. **T16**
21 Minto St. **N15**
7 Mitchell St. **O19**
19 Moat Dr. **J14**
19 Moat Ho. **J14**
19 Moat Pl. **J14**
19 Moat St. **J14**
19 Moat Terr. **J14**
15 Moira Terr. **Q17**
21 Moncreiff Terr. **N15**
21 Moncrieffe House **P12**
29 Monkbarns Gdns. **O12**
21 Monkwood Ct. **M14**
6 Monmouth Terr. **L18**
2 Montague St. **N15**
21 Montagu Terr. **L18**
13 Montgomery Pl. E. **N17**
13 Montgomery Pl. W. **N17**
13 Montgomery St. **N17**
13 Montgomery St. La. **N17**
20 Montpelier **L15**
20 Montpelier Park **L15**
20 Montpelier Terr. **L15**
13 Montrose Terr. **N17**
2 Moray House Coll. of
Education **N16**
1 Moray Pl. **L17**
30 Moredun Dykes Rd. **P11**
30 Moredun House **P12**
30 Moredun Institute
(Animal Diseases) **P12**
30 Moredun Park Ct. **P12**
30 Moredun Park Dr. **P12**
30 Moredun Park Gdns. **P12**
30 Moredun Park Gr. **Q12**
30 Moredun Park Gro. **Q12**
30 Moredun Park Loan **P12**
30 Moredun Park Rd. **P12**
30 Moredun Park St. **P12**
30 Moredun Park View **Q12**
30 Moredun Park Walk **Q12**
30 Moredun Park Way **P12**
30 Moredun Sch. **P12**
30 Moredunvale Bank **P12**
30 Moredunvale Gr. **P12**
30 Moredunvale Gro. **P12**
30 Moredunvale Loan **P12**
30 Moredunvale Park **P12**
30 Moredunvale Pl. **P12**
30 Moredunvale Rd. **P12**
30 Moredunvale View **P12**
30 Moredunvale Way **P12**
22 Morgan Athletic Grd.
O14
20 Morningside Cem. **L13**
20 Morningside Ct. **L13**
20 Morningside Dr. **K13**
20 Morningside Gdns. **K13**
20 Morningside Gro. **K13**
20 Morningside Park (street)
L14
20 Morningside Park **L13**
20 Morningside Pl. **L14**
20 Morningside Rd. **L14**
20 Morningside Terr. **L14**
1 Morrison St. **L16**
16 Morton St. **S16**
21 Mortonhall Cem. **N11**
29 Mortonhall Crem. **N11**
29 Mortonhall Garden Centre
N11

28 Mortonhall Golf Course
M12
29 Mortonhall Park Av. **N11**
29 Mortonhall Park Bk. **O11**
29 Mortonhall Park Cr. **O11**
29 Mortonhall Park Dr. **O11**
29 Mortonhall Park Gdns.
N11
29 Mortonhall Park Gr. **N11**
29 Mortonhall Park Gro. **N11**
29 Mortonhall Park Loan
N11
29 Mortonhall Park Pl. **O11**
29 Mortonhall Park View
N11
29 Mortonhall Park Way
N11
21 Mortonhall Rd. **M14**
9 Morven St. **F17**
Mossgiel Walk* =
Cumnor Cr.
21 Moston Terr. **N14**
1 Mound Pl. **M16**
1 Mound, The **M16**
16 Mount Lodge Pl. **R16**
1 Mount Royal Hotel **M16**
30 Mount Vernon Cem. **O12**
29 Mount Vernon Rd. **O12**
1 Mountbatten Bdg. **M16**
15 Mountcastle Bank **Q16**
15 Mountcastle Cr. **Q16**
15 Mountcastle Dr. N. **Q16**
15 Mountcastle Dr. S. **Q16**
15 Mountcastle Gdns. **Q16**
15 Mountcastle Gr. **Q17**
15 Mountcastle Gro. **Q16**
15 Mountcastle Loan **Q16**
Mountcastle Park* =
Mountcastle Cr.
15 Mountcastle Pl. **Q17**
15 Mountcastle Terr. **Q16**
11 Muirdale Terr. **H17**
26 Muirend Av. **G12**
5 Muirhouse Av. **H18**
4 Muirhouse Bank **H18**
4 Muirhouse Dr. **H19**
4 Muirhouse Gdns. **H19**
4 Muirhouse Gr. **H18**
4 Muirhouse Gro. **H19**
4 Muirhouse Loan **H19**
4 Muirhouse Medway **H18**
4 Muirhouse Park (street)
H18
4 Muirhouse Park **H19**
4 Muirhouse Parkway **H19**
5 Muirhouse Pl. E. **H18**
5 Muirhouse Pl. W. **H18**
5 Muirhouse Sch. **H18**
4 Muirhouse Terr. **H18**
4 Muirhouse View. **H19**
5 Muirhouse Way **H18**
25 Muirwood Cr. **E11**
25 Muirwood Dr. **E11**
25 Muirwood Gro. **E11**
25 Muirwood Pl. **E11**
25 Muirwood Rd. **E11**
Mulberry Pl.* =
Newhaven Rd.
26 Munro Dr. **H11**
Munro Pl.* = Canonmills
13 Murano Pl. **N17**
21 Murchison Ho. **N13**
21 Murdoch Terr. **L15**
12 Murieston Cr. **K15**
12 Murieston Cr. La. **K15**
12 Murieston La. **K15**
12 Murieston Pl. **K15**
12 Murieston Rd. **K15**
12 Murieston Terr. **K15**
Murray Cotts.* =
Ladywell Rd.
9 Murray Gr. **F15**
30 Murray Home **P12**
17 Murrayburn Appr. **F13**
17 Murrayburn Dr. **F13**
18 Murrayburn Gdns. **G13**
17 Murrayburn Gate **F13**

18 Murrayburn Gr. **G13**
18 Murrayburn Gro. **G13**
18 Murrayburn Pk. **F13**
18 Murrayburn Pl. **F13**
18 Murrayburn Rd. **F13**
18 Murrayburn Sch. **G13**
11 Murrayfield Av. **J16**
11 Murrayfield Dr. **J16**
11 Murrayfield Gdns. **J16**
11 Murrayfield Golf Course
H16
10 Murrayfield Hospital **H16**
Murrayfield Pl.* =
Coltbridge Av.
11 Murrayfield Rd. **J16**
11 Murrayfield Stadium **J15**
Museum of Childhood* =
High St.
1 Music Hall **M16**
16 Musselburgh Rd. **S16**
20 Myreside Ct. **K13**
20 Myreside Rd. **K14**
19 Myrtle Terr. **K15**

8 Nantwich Dr. **Q18**
20 Napier Coll. of Science
and Technology **L14**
20 Napier Rd. **K14**
1 National Gallery **M16**
2 National Library of
Scotland **M16**
2 National Museum of
Antiquities of Scotland
M17
30 Nellfield **O12**
Nelson Pl.* = Dublin
Meuse
1 Nelson St. **M17**
25 Nether Currie Cr. **E11**
25 Nether Currie Pl. **E11**
25 Nether Currie Rd. **E11**
25 Nether Currie Sch. **E11**
22 Nether Liberton **O13**
2 Netherbow Arts Centre
N16
6 Netherby Rd. **L19**
2 New Broughton **M17**
13 New College **M16**
7 New La. **M19**
19 New Market Rd. **J14**
19 New Markets **J14**
19 New Mart Rd. **H14**
2 New St. Andrews Ho.
M17
13 New St. **N16**
20 Newbattle Terr. **L14**
24 Newcraighall Ind. Estate
R14
24 Newcraighall Park **T14**
24 Newcraighall Rd. **R14**
24 Newcraighall Sch. **T14**
6 Newhaven Main St. **M20**
7 Newhaven Pl. **M20**
7 Newhaven Rd. **M19**
22 Newington Cem. **O14**
21 Newington Rd. **N15**
7 Newkirkgate **N18**
1 Newport St. **L16**
30 Newtoft St. **Q11**
31 Newton Church Rd. **S12**
19 Newton St. **K15**
31 Newton Village **S12**
7 Nicoll Pl. **N19**
2 Nicolson Sq. **N16**
2 Nicolson St. **N16**
24 Niddrie Cotts. **S14**
23 Niddrie Farm Gro. **Q14**
23 Niddrie House Av. **R14**
23 Niddrie House Dr. **R14**
23 Niddrie House Gdns. **R14**
29 Niddrie House Gro. **R14**
23 Niddrie House Park **Q14**
23 Niddrie House Sq. **Q14**
23 Niddrie Mains Dr. **R14**
23 Niddrie Mains Dr. **Q14**
23 Niddrie Mains Rd. **P14**

23 Niddrie Mains Terr. **Q14**
23 Niddrie Marischal Cr. **Q14**
23 Niddrie Marischal Dr. **Q14**
23 Niddrie Marischal Gdns. **Q14**
23 Niddrie Marischal Gr. **Q14**
23 Niddrie Marischal Gro. **R14**
23 Niddrie Marischal Loan **Q14**
23 Niddrie Marischal Pl. **Q14**
23 Niddrie Marischal Rd. **R14**
23 Niddrie Marischal St. **Q14**
23 Niddrie Mill Av. **R14**
23 Niddrie Mill Cr. **R15**
23 Niddrie Mill Dr. **R14**
23 Niddrie Mill Gro. **R14**
23 Niddrie Mill Pl. **R14**
23 Niddrie Mill Terr. **R14**
23 Niddrie Policies **R14**
23 Niddrie Sch. **Q14**
2 Niddry St. **M16**
Niddry St. S.* = Cowgate
29 Nigel Loan **O12**
20 Nile Gro. **L14**
8 Nisbet House **O18**
8 Noble Pl. **O18**
12 Normal Practising
Episcopal Sch. **K15**
13 North Bank St. **M16**
2 North Bridge **M16**
2 North British Hotel **M16**
9 North Bughtlin Bk. **E17**
9 North Bughtlin Brae **E17**
9 North Bughtlin Gate **E17**
9 North Bughtlin Neuk **E17**
9 North Bughtlin Pl. **E17**
9 North Bughtlin Rd. **E17**
9 North Bughtlinfield **E17**
9 North Bughtlinrig **E17**
9 North Bughtlinside **E17**
1 North Castle St. **L17**
1 North Charlotte St. **L16**
2 North Clyde St. La. **M17**
1 North East Circus Pl. **L17**
7 North Fort St. **N19**
23 North Greens **R15**
9 North Gyle Av. **E15**
9 North Gyle Dr. **E16**
9 North Gyle Farm Ct. **E15**
9 North Gyle Farm La. **E15**
9 North Gyle Gro. **E16**
9 North Gyle Loan **E16**
9 North Gyle Park **E16**
9 North Gyle Rd. **E16**
9 North Gyle Terr. **E15**
7 North Junction St. **N19**
13 North Meadow Walk **M15**
19 North Merchiston Cem. **K15**
12 North Park Terr. **L17**
North St. Andrew La.* = N. St. Andrew St.
2 North St. Andrew St. **M17**
13 North St. David St. **M17**
14 North Way, The **P16**
1 North West Circus Pl. **L17**
12 Northcote St. **K15**
5 Northern General Hosp. **K18**
14 Northfield Av. **P16**
15 Northfield Bdwy. **P17**
15 Northfield Circus **P16**
15 Northfield Cr. **P16**
15 Northfield Dr. **Q16**
15 Northfield Farm Av. **Q16**
15 Northfield Farm Rd. **Q16**
15 Northfield Gdns. **Q16**
15 Northfield Gro. **Q16**
15 Northfield Park **Q16**
15 Northfield Park Gro. **Q16**
15 Northfield Rd. **P16**
15 Northfield Sq. **Q16**
Northfield Terr.* = Willowbrae Rd.
4 Northlawn Terr. **G18**

Northumberland Pl.* = Northumberland St.
1 Northumberland Pl. La. **M17**
13 Northumberland St. **M17**
1 Northumberland St. La., N.E. **M17**
1 Northumberland St. La., N.W. **M17**
1 Northumberland St. La., S.E. **M17**
1 Northumberland St. La., S.W. **M17**
5 Northview Ct. **H19**
14 Norton Park **O17**
2 Nottingham Pl. **N17**
Nottingham Terr.* = Nottingham Pl.
10 Oak La. **G17**
8 Oakville Terr. **O18**
21 Observatory Rd. **N13**
22 Ochiltree Gdns. **P13**
2 Odeon Cinema **N15**
20 Ogilvie Terr. **K14**
Old Assembly Cl.* = High St.
2 Old Broughton **M17**
29 Old Burdiehouse Rd. **O10**
14 Old Church La. **P15**
2 Old Dalkeith Rd. **O14**
27 Old Farm Av. **J12**
27 Old Farm Pl. **H12**
2 Old Fishmarket Cl. **M16**
22 Old Kirk Rd. **G16**
22 Old Mill La. **O13**
Old Quadrangle* = South Bridge
2 Old Tolbooth Wynd **N16**
2 Old Waverley Hotel **M16**
11 Orchard Bank **K17**
12 Orchard Brae **K17**
11 Orchard Brae Av. **K17**
11 Orchard Brae Gdns. **K17**
11 Orchard Brae Gdns. W. **K17**
12 Orchard Brae Ho. **K17**
Orchard Brae West* = Orchard Brae
11 Orchard Cr. **J17**
11 Orchard Dr. **J17**
11 Orchard Gdns. **J17**
12 Orchard Gro. **K17**
12 Orchard Pl. **K17**
11 Orchard Rd. **K17**
11 Orchard Rd. S. **J17**
11 Orchard Terr. **K17**
11 Orchard Toll **K17**
17 Orchardfield Av. **F15**
7 Orchardfield La. **N18**
29 Orchardhead Loan **O12**
27 Orchardhead Rd. **O12**
16 Ormelie Terr. **S16**
16 Ormidale Terr. **J16**
10 Ormiston Terr. **F15**
27 Orwell Pl. **K15**
12 Orwell Terr. **K15**
26 Osborne Terr. **K16**
21 Oswald Ct. **M14**
21 Oswald Rd. **M14**
27 Oswald Terr. **F15**
19 Otterburn Pk **J12**
4 Oxcars Ct. **H19**
13 Oxford St. **N15**
12 Oxford Terr. **L17**
27 Oxgangs Av. **K11**
27 Oxgangs Bank **K11**
27 Oxgangs Bdwy. **K11**
27 Oxgangs Cr. **K12**
27 Oxgangs Dr. **K12**
27 Oxgangs Farm Av. **K11**
27 Oxgangs Farm Dr. **K11**
27 Oxgangs Farm Gdns. **K11**
27 Oxgangs Farm Gro. **K11**
27 Oxgangs Farm Loan **K11**
27 Oxgangs Farm Terr. **K11**
27 Oxgangs Gdns. **K12**

27 Oxgangs Gr. **K12**
27 Oxgangs Gro. **K12**
27 Oxgangs Hill **K12**
27 Oxgangs Ho. **K12**
28 Oxgangs Loan **K12**
27 Oxgangs Medway **K11**
27 Oxgangs Park **K11**
27 Oxgangs Path **K11**
27 Oxgangs Path E. **K11**
27 Oxgangs Pl. **K12**
27 Oxgangs Rise **K12**
27 Oxgangs Rd. **K11**
27 Oxgangs Rd. N. **J12**
27 Oxgangs Row **K11**
27 Oxgangs Sch. **J12**
27 Oxgangs St.* **K11**
27 Oxgangs Terr. **K11**
27 Oxgangs View **K11**

10 Paddock Holm **G15**
14 Paisley Av. **P16**
14 Paisley Cr. **P16**
14 Paisley Dr. **P16**
14 Paisley Gdns. **P16**
14 Paisley Gro. **P16**
14 Paisley Terr. **P16**
25 Palmer Pl. **D10**
25 Palmer Rd. **D11**
12 Palmerston Pl. **L16**
Palmerston Pl. La.* = Palmerston Pl.
21 Palmerston Rd. **M15**
1 Panmure Pl. **M15**
15 Park Av. **R16**
22 Park Ct. **K13**
29 Park Cr. **O12**
20 Park Gdns. **O12**
22 Park Gro. **O12**
6 Park Pl. **M19**
6 Park Rd. **M19**
24 Park Terr. **T14**
24 Park View **S14**
15 Parker Av. **Q17**
15 Parker Rd. **Q17**
15 Parker Terr. **Q17**
9 Parkgrove Av. **F17**
9 Parkgrove Bank **F17**
9 Parkgrove Cr. **F17**
9 Parkgrove Dr. **F17**
9 Parkgrove Gdns. **F17**
9 Parkgrove Gr. **F17**
9 Parkgrove Loan **F17**
9 Parkgrove Neuk **F17**
Parkgrove Path* = Parkgrove Terr.
9 Parkgrove Pl. **F17**
9 Parkgrove Rd. **F17**
9 Parkgrove Row **F17**
9 Parkgrove St. **F17**
9 Parkgrove Terr. **F17**
9 Parkgrove View **F17**
18 Parkhead Av. **G13**
18 Parkhead Cr. **G13**
18 Parkhead Dr. **G13**
18 Parkhead Gdns. **G13**
18 Parkhead Gro. **G13**
18 Parkhead Loan **G13**
18 Parkhead Pl. **G13**
18 Parkhead St. **G13**
18 Parkhead Terr. **G13**
18 Parkhead View **G13**
2 Parkside St. **N15**
13 Parkside Terr. **N15**
8 Parkvale Pl. **O18**
2 Parliament House **M16**
Parliament Pl.* = Parliament St.
2 Parliament Sq. **M16**
2 Parliament St. **N19**
23 Parrotshot **R15**
14 Parsons Green Sch. **P16**
14 Parsons Green Terr. **P17**
27 Patie's Rd. **J12**
26 Paties Rd. Sports Grd. **H12**
Patriothall* = Hamilton Pl.

8 Pattison St. **O19**
24 Peacocktail Cl. **R14**
9 Pearce Av. **F16**
9 Pearce Gro. **F16**
9 Pearce Rd. **F16**
18 Peatville Gdns. **H13**
18 Peatville Terr. **H13**
21 Peel Terr. **N14**
22 Peffer Bank **P14**
22 Peffer Pl. **P14**
22 Peffer St. **P14**
22 Peffermill Ct. **P14**
22 Peffermill House **P14**
22 Peffermill Rd. **O14**
23 Peffermill Sch. **P14**
3 Peggy's Mill Rd. **E18**
12 Pembroke Pl. **K16**
5 Pennywell Cotts. **H19**
5 Pennywell Ct. **H19**
4 Pennywell Gdns. **H19**
4 Pennywell Gro. **H19**
4 Pennywell Medway **H19**
4 Pennywell Pl. **H19**
5 Pennywell Rd. **H19**
5 Pennywell Villas **H19**
26 Pentland Av. **H12**
28 Pentland Cr. **L12**
28 Pentland Dr. **K11**
28 Pentland Gdns. **L12**
28 Pentland Gro. **L12**
26 Pentland Hills **F10**
19 Pentland Ho. **J14**
25 Pentland Pl. **D10**
26 Pentland Rd. **H12**
28 Pentland Terr. **L12**
28 Pentland View, Comiston **L11**
25 Pentland View, Currie **D10**
25 Pentland View Ct. **E10**
13 Perth St. **L17**
29 Peveril Terr. **O12**
2 Picardy Pl. **M17**
9 Pier Pl. **M20**
14 Piersfield Gro. **P17**
14 Piersfield Pl. **P17**
14 Piersfield Terr. **P17**
15 Piershill Cem. **Q17**
14 Piershill La. **P17**
14 Piershill Pl. **P17**
14 Piershill Sq. E. **P17**
14 Piershill Sq. W. **P17**
14 Piershill Terr. **P17**
30 Pillars, The **P12**
7 Pilrig Cotts. **N18**
7 Pilrig Gdns. **N18**
Pilrig House Ct.* = Bonnington Rd.
7 Pilrig Park **N18**
7 Pilrig Park Sch. **N18**
Pilrig Pl.* = Pilrig St.
7 Pilrig St. **N18**
5 Pilton Av. **K19**
5 Pilton Cr. **K19**
5 Pilton Dr. **K19**
5 Pilton Dr. N. **K19**
5 Pilton Gdns. **K19**
5 Pilton Loan **K19**
5 Pilton Park **K19**
5 Pilton Pl. **K19**
15 Pipe La. **R17**
15 Pipe St. **R17**
8 Pirniefield Bank **P18**
8 Pirniefield Gdns. **P18**
8 Pirniefield Gro. **P18**
8 Pirniefield Pl. **P18**
8 Pirniefield Terr. **P18**
5 Pirniehall Sch. **J19**
7 Pirrie St. **N18**
14 Pitlochry Pl. **O17**
20 Pitsligo Rd. **L14**
5 Pitt St. **N19**
16 Pittville St. **R16**
16 Pittville St. La. **R16**
Playfair Steps* = N. Bank St.
2 Playhouse **N17**
2 Pleasance **N16**

2 Pleasance Thea. N16
20 Plewlands Av. K13
20 Plewlands Ct. K13
20 Plewlands Gdns. K13
20 Plewlands Terr. K13
29 Pleydell Pl. O12
22 Pollock Halls O15
20 Polwarth Cr. L15
20 Polwarth Gdns. K15
20 Polwarth Gro. K15
20 Polwarth Park K15
20 Polwarth Pl. K15
20 Polwarth Terr. K14
1 Ponton St. L15
8 Poplar La. O19
5 Porterfield Rd. K18
12 Portgower Pl. L17
Portland Pl.* =
  North Junction St.
Portland Terr.* =
  North Junction St.
7 Portland St. N19
16 Portobello Cem. T16
15 Portobello Golf Course
  R16
15 Portobello High St. R17
15 Portobello Rd. P17
15 Portobello Sch. Q16
15 Portobello Sch. Annexe
  R16
Portsburgh Sq.* =
  West Port
10 Post House Hotel G15
2 Post Office M16
2 Potterrow M16
2 Powderhall Stadium M18
21 Preston St. Sch. N15
22 Prestonfield Av. O14
22 Prestonfield Cr. O14
22 Prestonfield Gdns. O14
22 Prestonfield Golf Course
  O15
22 Prestonfield Park O14
22 Prestonfield Rd. O14
22 Prestonfield Sch. O14
22 Prestonfield Terr. O14
22 Priestfield Av. O14
22 Priestfield Cr. O14
22 Priestfield Gdns. O14
22 Priestfield Gro. O15
22 Priestfield Rd. O15
22 Priestfield Rd. N. O15
7 Primrose St. O18
19 Primrose Terr. K15
6 Primrose Bank Rd. L19
7 Prince Regent St. N19
1 Princes St. L16
1 Princess Alexandra Eye
  Pavilion M15
28 Princess Margaret Rose
  Hosp. M11
16 Promenade R17
13 Prospect Bank M17
8 Prospect Bank Cr. O18
8 Prospect Bank Gdns.
  O18
8 Prospect Bank Gro. R18
8 Prospect Bank Pl. P18
8 Prospect Bank Rd. O18
8 Prospect Bank Sch. O18
13 Prospect Bank Sch.
  (Primary)M17
8 Prospect Bank Terr. P18

4 Quality St. G18
4 Quality St. La. G18
13 Quarry Cl. N15
24 Quarry Cotts. R14
7 Quayside St. N19
Queen Charlotte La.* =
  Queen Charlotte St.
7 Queen Charlotte St. O19
10 Queen Margaret Coll.
  F16
1 Queen St. L17
1 Queen St. Gdns. M17

1 Queen St. Gdns. E. M17
1 Queen St. Gdns. W.
  17
11 Queen's Av. H17
11 Queen's Av. S. J17
16 Queen's Bay Cr. S16
21 Queen's Cr. N14
14 Queen's Drive O16
11 Queen's Gdns. J17
13 Queen's Hall, The N15
14 Queen's Park Av. O17
13 Queen's Pl. N17
11 Queen's Rd. J17
23 Queen's Walk Q14
3 Queensferry Rd. E14
1 Queensferry St. L16
1 Queensferry St. La. L16
11 Queensferry Terr. K17
7 Quilts, The N19

12 Raeburn Pl. L17
12 Raeburn St. L17
15 Ramsey Annexe
  (Stevenson Coll.) Q17
1 Ramsay Gdn. M16
1 Ramsay La. M16
15 Ramsay Pl. R17
1 Randolph Cliff L16
1 Randolph Cr. L16
1 Randolph Hall L16
1 Randolph La. L16
1 Randolph Pl. L16
2 Rankeillor St. N15
21 Rankin Av. N13
21 Rankin Dr. N13
21 Rankin Rd. N14
10 Rannoch Gro. F17
10 Rannoch Pl. F17
10 Rannoch Rd. F17
9 Rannoch Terr. F17
8 Ransome Gdns. F17
21 Ratcliffe Terr. N14
15 Rathbone Pl. R17
1 Ravelston Ct. J16
11 Ravelston Dykes J16
11 Ravelston Dykes La. H16
11 Ravelston Dykes Rd. H17
11 Ravelston Gdn. J16
11 Ravelston Golf Course
  H17
11 Ravelston Heights J17
11 Ravelston House Gro.
  J17
11 Ravelston House Loan
  J17
11 Ravelston House Park
  J17
11 Ravelston House Rd.
  J17
11 Ravelston Pk. (st) K16
11 Ravelston Park H17
Ravelston Pl.* =
  Belford Rd.
11 Ravelston Rise J16
12 Ravelston Terr. K17
30 Ravenscroft Gdns. Q11
30 Ravenscroft Pl. Q11
30 Ravenscroft St. Q11
22 Ravenswood Av. O13
7 Redbraes Gro. M18
7 Redbraes Park M18
7 Redbraes Pl. M18
27 Redford Av. J11
27 Redford Bank J11
27 Redford Barracks J12
27 Redford Cr. J11
27 Redford Dr. H11
27 Redford Gdns. J11
27 Redford Gro. J12
27 Redford Loan J11
27 Redford Neuk J11
27 Redford Pl. J12
27 Redford Rd. J11
27 Redford Terr. J11
27 Redford Walk J11
22 Redgauntlet Terr. P13

18 Redhall Av. H13
18 Redhall Bank Rd. H13
18 Redhall Cr. H13
18 Redhall Dr. H13
18 Redhall Gdns. H13
18 Redhall Gro. H13
19 Redhall House Dr. H13
18 Redhall Park H13
18 Redhall Pl. H13
18 Redhall Rd. H13
18 Redhall View H13
17 Redheughs Road D15
Regent Bridge* =
  Waterloo Pl.
2 Regent Gardens N17
14 Regent Pl. O17
2 Regent Pl. N16
2 Regent Road Park N17
16 Regent St. R16
16 Regent St. La. R16
2 Regent Terr. N17
2 Regent Terr. La. N17
Regent Terr. Mews* =
  Regent Terr. La.
3 Regis St. E18
2 Register House M17
2 Register Pl. M17
12 Reid Terr. L17
2 Reid's Cl. N16
Reid's Ct.* = Canongate
21 Relugas Gdns. N14
21 Relugas Pl. N14
21 Relugas Rd. N14
14 Restalrig Av. P17
8 Restalrig Circus P18
8 Restalrig Cr. P18
14 Restalrig Dr. P17
14 Restalrig Gdns. P17
14 Restalrig House P17
8 Restalrig Park O18
14 Restalrig Rd. O18
14 Restalrig Rd. S. P17
14 Restalrig Sch. P17
8 Restalrig Sq. P18
7 Restalrig Terr. O18
25 Riccarton Av. D11
25 Riccarton Cr. E11
25 Riccarton Dr. D11
25 Riccarton Gro. E11
25 Riccarton Mains Rd. E11
25 Riccarton Sch. D10
2 Richmond La. N16
2 Richmond Pl. N16
2 Richmond Terr. L16
3 Riding Park E18
13 Rillbank Cr. M15
13 Rillbank Terr. M15
29 Ringwood Pl. O12
12 Rintoul Pl. L17
28 Riselaw Cr. L12
28 Riselaw Pl. L12
28 Riselaw Rd. L12
28 Riselaw Terr. L12
20 Ritchie Pl. K15
11 Riversdale Cr. J15
11 Riversdale Gro. J16
11 Riversdale Rd. J16
19 Robb's Loan J14
19 Robb's Loan Gro. J14
22 Robert Burns Dr. O13
19 Robertson Av. J15
2 Robertson's Cl. N16
5 Rocheid Park K18
6 Rocheid Path K18
20 Rochester Terr. L14
13 Rodney St. M17
Ronaldson's Wharf* =
  Sandport Pl.
1 Rose St. L16
1 Rose St. La., N. L16
1 Rose St. La., S. L16
1 Rosebank Cem. N18
1 Rosebank Cotts. L16
6 Rosebank Gdns. L19
6 Rosebank Gro. L19
6 Rosebank Rd. L19
12 Rosebery Cr. K16
12 Rosebery Cr. La. K16

12 Rosebery Ho. K16
11 Roseburn Av. J16
11 Roseburn Cliff K16
11 Roseburn Cr. J16
11 Roseburn Dr. J16
11 Roseburn Gdns. J16
11 Roseburn Park J16
11 Roseburn Pl. J16
11 Roseburn Sch. J15
11 Roseburn St. J15
11 Roseburn Terr. J16
15 Rosefield Av. R16
15 Rosefield Av. La. R16
15 Rosefield La. R16
15 Rosefield Park R16
15 Rosefield Pl. R16
15 Rosefield St. R16
1 Rosemount Bdgs. L16
21 Roseneath Pl. M15
21 Roseneath St. M15
21 Roseneath Terr. M15
8 Rosevale Pl. O18
8 Rosevale Terr. O18
6 Roseville Gdns. M19
21 Ross Gdns. N14
21 Ross Pl. N14
22 Ross Rd. N13
14 Rossie Pl. O17
7 Rosslyn Cr. N18
7 Rosslyn Terr. N18
12 Rothesay Mews K16
12 Rothesay Pl. L16
12 Rothesay Terr. L16
18 Roull Gro. F15
18 Roull Pl. F15
18 Roull Rd. F15
2 Roxburgh Pl. N16
2 Roxburgh St. N16
Roxburgh Terr.* =
  Drummond St.
2 Roxburghe Hotel L16
2 Royal Bank M17
6 Royal Botanic Gdn. L18
2 Royal British Hotel M16
3 Royal Burgess Golf
  Course E18
1 Royal Circus L17
21 Royal Commonwealth
  Pool N15
13 Royal Cr. M17
21 Royal (Dick) Veterinary
  Coll. N15
20 Royal Edinburgh Hosp.
  L14
4 Royal High Sch., The F18
14 Royal High Sch., The
  (Primary) P16
21 Royal Hospital for Sick
  Children M15
2 Royal Infirmary M15
2 Royal Mile Sch. N16
21 Royal Observatory M13
14 Royal Park Pl. O17
14 Royal Park Terr. O17
9 Royal Scot Hotel E15
1 Royal Scottish Academy
  M16
2 Royal Scottish Museum
  M16
2 Royal Terr. N17
2 Royal Terrace Gdns. N17
Royal Terrace Mews* =
  Regent Terr. La.
11 Royal Victoria Hosp. K17
5 Royston Mains Av. J19
5 Royston Mains Cr. J19
5 Royston Mains Gdns.
  K19
5 Royston Mains Gr. K19
5 Royston Mains Pl. J19
5 Royston Mains Rd. K19
5 Royston Mains St. J19
5 Royston Sch. K19
6 Royston Terr. L18
20 Rudolph Steiner Sch.
  K14
6 Russell Pl. L19
11 Russell Rd. K16

Rustic Cotts.* = Colinton Rd.
22 Rutherford Dr. **O13**
1 Rutland Ct. **L16**
Rutland Pl.* = West End
1 Rutland Sq. **L16**
1 Rutland St. **L16**
8 Ryehill Av. **O18**
8 Ryehill Gdns. **O18**
8 Ryehill Gro. **O18**
8 Ryehill Pl. **O18**
8 Ryehill Terr. **O18**

22 Saddletree Loan **P13**
4 Safeway Shopping Centre **G18**
14 Safeway Shopping Centre **P17**
21 St. Alban's Rd. **M14**
7 St. Andrew Pl. **O18**
2 St. Andrew Sq. **M17**
19 St. Andrew's Coll. of Educ. **J13**
2 St. Andrew's Hotel **M17**
2 St. Andrew's House **N17**
St. Anthony Ct.* = St. Anthony St.
St. Anthony La.* = St. Anthony St.
7 St. Anthony Pl. **N19**
7 St. Anthony St. **N19**
17 St. Augustine's Sch. **F14**
30 St. Barnabas Ct. **Q12**
1 St. Bernard's Cr. **L17**
St. Bernard's Pl.* = Saunders St.
12 St. Bernard's Row **L17**
10 St. Catherine's Gdns. **H15**
21 St. Catherine's Pl. **N15**
30 St. Catherine's Sch. **O11**
2 St. Cecilia's Hall **N16**
23 St. Christopher's Sch. **R15**
7 St. Clair Av. **O18**
7 St. Clair Pl. **O18**
7 St. Clair Rd. **O18**
7 St. Clair St. **O18**
20 St. Clair Terr. **K13**
1 St. Colme St. **L16**
13 St. Colm's Coll. **L18**
6 St. Columba's Hospice **L19**
21 St. Crispin's Sch. **N14**
19 St. Cuthbert's Sch. **J14**
St. David's Pl.* = Morrison St
St. David's Terr.* = Morrison St.
20 St. Denis and Cranley Sch. **K14**
20 St. Fillan's Terr. **L13**
23 St. Francis' Sch. **Q14**
11 St. George's Sch. **K16**
2 St. Giles' Cathedral **M16**
17 St. Giles' Sch. **F13**
2 St. Giles' St. **M16**
2 St. James Centre **M17**
2 St. John St. **N16**
22 St. John Vianney Sch. **O13**
10 St. John's Av. **G15**
10 St. John's Cr. **G15**
10 St. John's Gdns. **G15**
St. John's Pl.* = Holyrood Rd.
9 St. John's Rd. **F15**
15 St. John's Sch. **R16**
10 St. John's Terr. **G15**
2 St. Joseph's Sch. **G14**
29 St. Katharine's Brae **O11**
29 St. Katharine's Cr. **O11**
29 St. Katharine's Loan **O11**
2 St. Leonard's Bank **N15**
2 St. Leonard's Hill **N15**
2 St. Leonard's La. **N15**

13 St. Leonard's St. **N15**
21 St. Margaret's Convent Sch. **M14**
9 St. Margaret's Park **F15**
21 St. Margaret's Rd. **L14**
20 St. Margaret's Sch. **L13**
22 St. Margaret's Sch. **O14**
16 St. Mark's La. **R16**
7 St. Mark's Park **M18**
16 St. Mark's Pl. **R16**
27 St. Mark's Sch. **K12**
1 St. Mary's Cathedral (Episc). **L16**
2 St. Mary's Cathedral (R.C.) **M17**
1 St. Mary's Cathedral Choir Sch. **L16**
16 St. Mary's Pl. **S16**
2 St. Mary's Sch. **M17**
7 St. Mary's Sch., Leith **N19**
2 St. Mary's St. **N16**
19 St. Nicholas' Sch. **J15**
9 St. Ninian's Dr. **F16**
10 St. Ninian's Rd. **F16**
14 St. Ninian's Sch. **P17**
20 St. Ninian's Terr. **K13**
2 St. Patrick Sq. **N15**
2 St. Patrick St. **N15**
St. Patrick Sch.* = Cowgate
2 St. Patrick's Sch. **N16**
St. Peter's Bdgs.* = Gilmore Pl.
12 St. Peter's Pl. **L15**
20 St. Peter's Sch. **L14**
13 St. Peter's Sch. Annexe **M15**
21 St. Raphael's Hosp. **M14**
20 St. Ronan's Terr. **L13**
11 St. Serf's Sch. **K16**
St. Stephen Pl* = St. Stephen St.
2 St. Stephen St **L17**
1 St. Thomas of Aquin's Sch. **M15**
21 St. Thomas Rd. **M14**
1 St. Vincent St. **L17**
1 Salamander Pl. **O19**
8 Salamander St. **O19**
21 Salisbury Pl. **N15**
21 Salisbury Rd. **N15**
14 Salmond Pl. **O17**
1 Saltire Society **L16**
4 Salvesen Cr. **H19**
4 Salvesen Gdns. **H19**
4 Salvesen Gro. **H19**
4 Salvesen Terr. **H19**
15 Sandford Gdns. **R16**
7 Sandport Pl. **N19**
7 Sandport St. **N19**
19 Saughton Av. **J14**
16 Saughton Cem. **H14**
10 Saughton Cr. **H15**
10 Saughton Gdns. **H15**
10 Saughton Gro. **H15**
10 Saughton Loan **H15**
18 Saughton Mains Av. **G14**
18 Saughton Mains Bank **H14**
Saughton Mains Cotts.* = Saughton Mains Gdns.
18 Saughton Mains Dr. **G14**
18 Saughton Mains Gdns. **G14**
18 Saughton Mains Gro. **H14**
18 Saughton Mains Loan **G14**
18 Saughton Mains Park **G14**
18 Saughton Mains Pl. **G14**
18 Saughton Mains St. **G14**
18 Saughton Mains Terr. **G14**
10 Saughton Park (st.) **H15**
19 Saughton Park **H15**
18 Saughton Prison **H14**
18 Saughton Rd. **G14**

18 Saughton Rd. N. **G15**
11 Saughtonhall Av. **H15**
11 Saughtonhall Av. W. **H15**
11 Saughtonhall Circus **J15**
11 Saughtonhall Cr. **H15**
11 Saughtonhall Dr. **H15**
11 Saughtonhall Gdns. **J15**
11 Saughtonhall Gro. **J15**
11 Saughtonhall Pl. **H15**
11 Saughtonhall Terr. **J15**
12 Saunders St. **L17**
21 Savile Pl. **N14**
21 Savile Terr. **N14**
12 Saxe-Coburg Pl. **L17**
12 Saxe-Coburg St. **L17**
Saxe-Coburg Terr.* = Saxe-Coburg St.
3 School Brae **E19**
21 Sciennes **N15**
21 Sciennes Gdns. **N15**
Sciennes Hill Pl.* = Sciennes
Sciennes House Dr.* = Sciennes
21 Sciennes House Pl. **N15**
21 Sciennes Pl. **N15**
21 Sciennes Rd. **M15**
21 Sciennes Sch. **M15**
Sciennes St. E.* = Causewayside
14 Scone Gdns. **P17**
1 Scotia Hotel **M17**
13 Scotland St. **M17**
13 Scotland St. La. **M17**
2 Scott Monument **M16**
1 Scottish Experience, The **L16**
6 Scottish National Gall. of Modern Art **K16**
2 Scottish National Portrait Gall. **M17**
13 Scottish Widows **N15**
20 Scottish Youth Hostel Association Office **L15**
10 Scottish Zoological Park **G16**
8 Seafield Av. **P18**
8 Seafield Cem. **P18**
8 Seafield Crem. **P18**
15 Seafield Ind. Estate **Q17**
8 Seafield Pl. **P18**
8 Seafield Recreation Grd. **Q18**
8 Seafield Rd. **P18**
8 Seafield Rd. E. **Q18**
8 Seafield St. **P18**
8 Seafield Way **Q18**
11 Seaforth Dr. **J17**
11 Seaforth Terr. **J17**
Seaport St.* = Bernard St.
16 Seaview Cr. **S16**
16 Seaview Terr. **S16**
1 Semple St. **L16**
21 Seton Pl. **N15**
19 Shaftesbury Park **K14**
19 Shandon Cr. **K14**
19 Shandon Pl. **K14**
19 Shandon Rd. **K14**
19 Shandon St. **K14**
19 Shandon Terr. **K14**
1 Shandwick Pl. **L16**
22 Shanter Way **O13**
9 Shaw's Pl. **N18**
Shaw's Sq.* = Gayfield Sq.
7 Shaw's St. **N18**
7 Shaw's Terr. **N18**
1 Sheraton **L16**
19 Sheriff Brae **N19**
2 Sheriff Court **M16**
7 Shore **O19**
7 Shore Pl. **O19**
13 Shrub Pl. **N17**
Shrub Pl. La.* = Shrub Pl.
18 Sighthill Av. **G13**
17 Sighthill Bank **F13**

17 Sighthill Ct. **F13**
17 Sighthill Cr. **F13**
17 Sighthill Dr. **F13**
18 Sighthill Gdns. **F13**
17 Sighthill Gr. **F13**
18 Sighthill Gro. **G13**
17 Sighthill Ind. Estate **E14**
17 Sighthill Loan **F13**
17 Sighthill Neuk **F13**
18 Sighthill Park (st.) **F13**
18 Sighthill Park **F14**
17 Sighthill Pl. **F13**
17 Sighthill Rise **F13**
17 Sighthill Rd. **F13**
17 Sighthill Sch. **F13**
17 Sighthill St. **F13**
18 Sighthill Terr. **F13**
17 Sighthill View **F13**
17 Sighthill Wynd **F13**
4 Silverknowes Av. **G18**
4 Silverknowes Bank **G18**
4 Silverknowes Brae **G18**
4 Silverknowes Ct. **G18**
4 Silverknowes Cr. **G18**
4 Silverknowes Dell **G18**
4 Silverknowes Dr. **G18**
4 Silverknowes Eastway **G18**
4 Silverknowes Gdns. **G19**
4 Silverknowes Golf Course **G19**
4 Silverknowes Gr. **H18**
4 Silverknowes Gro. **G19**
4 Silverknowes Hill **G18**
4 Silverknowes Loan **G18**
4 Silverknowes Midway **H18**
4 Silverknowes Neuk **H18**
4 Silverknowes Park **H18**
4 Silverknowes Parkway **G19**
4 Silverknowes Pl. **G19**
4 Silverknowes Rd. **G19**
4 Silverknowes Rd. E. **G18**
4 Silverknowes Rd. S. **G18**
4 Silverknowes Sch. **H18**
4 Silverknowes Southway **H18**
4 Silverknowes Terr. **G18**
4 Silverknowes View **H18**
2 Simon Sq. **N16**
1 Simpson Memorial Maternity Pavilion **M15**
19 Slateford Rd. **J14**
19 Slateford Sta. **J14**
14 Sleigh Dr. **O17**
14 Sleigh Gdns. **P17**
7 Sloan St. **N18**
19 Smithfield St. **J15**
7 Smith's Pl. **N18**
31 Smithy Green Av. **R12**
Solicitor's Bdgs.* = Cowgate
8 Somerset Pl. **O18**
18 South Barnton Av. **G18**
2 South Bridge **M16**
1 South Charlotte St. **L16**
13 South Clerk St. **N15**
1 South East Circus Pl. **L17**
7 South Fort St. **N19**
South Gayfield La.* = Gayfield Sq.
20 South Gillsland Rd **K14**
21 South Gray St. **N14**
2 South Gray's Cl. **N16**
11 South Groathill Av. **J17**
17 South Gyle Access **F14**
17 South Gyle Broadway **E14**
17 South Gyle Cres. **E14**
17 South Gyle Gdns. **E15**
17 South Gyle Ln. **E15**
17 South Gyle Pk. **E15**
17 South Gyle Rd. **F15**

17 South Gyle Wynd **F14**
21 South Lauder Road **N14**
6 South Laverockbank Av. **M19**
12 South Learmonth Av. **K17**
12 South Learmonth Gdns. **K17**
7 South Lorne Pl. **N18**
South Meadow Walk.* = Meadow Pl.
20 South Morningside Sch. **L13**
16 South Morton St. **S16**
21 South Oswald Rd. **M14**
21 South Oxford St. **N15**
6 South Pk. **M19**
2 South St. Andrew St. **M17**
2 South St. David St. **M16**
7 South Sloan St. **N18**
6 South Trinity Rd. **L19**
15 Southfield Bank **Q15**
15 Southfield Farm Gro. **Q16**
15 Southfield Gdns. E. **Q16**
15 Southfield Gdns. W. **Q16**
30 Southfield Hosp. **P12**
15 Southfield Loan **Q15**
15 Southfield Park **Q15**
15 Southfield Pl. **R16**
Southfield Pl. N.* = Southfield Sq.
Southfield Pl. S.* = Southfield Sq.
15 Southfield Rd. E. **Q15**
15 Southfield Rd. W. **Q15**
15 Southfield Sq. **Q15**
15 Southfield Terr. **Q15**
Southfield Villas.* = Stanley St.
29 Southhouse Av. **O11**
29 Southhouse Bdwy. **O10**
30 Southhouse Cr. **O10**
29 Southhouse Gdns. **O10**
29 Southhouse Gro. **O10**
30 Southhouse Medway **O11**
29 Southhouse Paths **O11**
29 Southhouse Rd. **O11**
30 Southhouse Sq. **O10**
30 Southhouse Terr. **P11**
30 Soutra Ct. **O11**
22 Spence St. **N15**
6 Spencer Pl. **L19**
7 Spey St. **N18**
7 Spey St. La. **N18**
7 Spey Terr. **N18**
7 Spiers Pl. **N19**
30 Spinney, The **P11**
1 Spittal St. **L16**
Spittalfield Cr.* = St. Leonard's St.
21 Spottiswoode Rd. **M15**
21 Spottiswoode St. **M15**
14 Spring Gdns. **O17**
Springfield Bdgs.* = Springfield St.
7 Springfield St. **N18**
20 Springvalley Gdns. **L14**
20 Springvalley Terr. **L14**
12 Springwell Pl. **K15**
29 Springwood Park **O12**
26 Spylaw Av. **G12**
26 Spylaw Bank Rd. **G12**
26 Spylaw Park (street) **G12**
26 Spylaw Park **H11**
20 Spylaw Rd. **K14**
26 Spylaw St. **H11**
20 Stable La. **L14**
1 Stafford St. **L16**
29 Stanedykehead **N11**
12 Stanhope Pl. **K16**
Stanhope Pl. West* = Stanhope Pl.
12 Stanhope St. **K16**
14 Stanley Pl. **O17**

6 Stanley Rd. **M19**
15 Stanley St. **R16**
7 Stanwell St. **N18**
6 Stapeley Av. **Q17**
6 Starbank Park **M19**
6 Starbank Rd. **M19**
27 Stark's Cotts. **K12**
10 Station Rd. **G15**
7 Stead's Pl. **N18**
5 Steel's Pl. **L14**
18 Stenhouse Av. **H14**
18 Stenhouse Av. W. **H14**
18 Stenhouse Cotts., **H14**
18 Stenhouse Cr. **H14**
18 Stenhouse Cross **H14**
18 Stenhouse Dr. **G14**
18 Stenhouse Gdns. **H14**
18 Stenhouse Gdns. N. **H14**
18 Stenhouse Gro. **H14**
18 Stenhouse Mill Cr. **H14**
18 Stenhouse Mill La. **H14**
18 Stenhouse Mill Wynd **H14**
18 Stenhouse Pl. E. **H14**
18 Stenhouse Pl. W. **H14**
18 Stenhouse Rd. **H14**
18 Stenhouse Sch. **H14**
18 Stenhouse St. E. **H14**
18 Stenhouse St. W. **G14**
18 Stenhouse Terr. **H14**
Stevenlaw's Cl.* = High St.
19 Stevenson Av. **J15**
17 Stevenson Coll. of Further Education **F14**
19 Stevenson Dr. **H14**
19 Stevenson Gro. **J15**
19 Stevenson Rd. **J15**
19 Stevenson Terr. **J15**
19 Stewart Terr. **J15**
12 Stewart's Melville Coll. **K17**
6 Stewart's Melville Coll. Sports Ground **K18**
9 Stirling Rd. **L19**
12 Stockbridge Sch. **L17**
Storrie's Alley* = Giles St.
11 Strachan Gdns. **H17**
11 Strachan Rd. **H17**
16 Straiton Pl. **R16**
29 Straiton Rd. **O10**
3 Strathalmond Ct. **D18**
3 Strathalmond Gr. **D18**
3 Strathalmond Park **D17**
3 Strathalmond Rd. **D17**
20 Strathearn Pl. **L14**
21 Strathearn Rd. **M14**
21 Strathfillan Rd. **M14**
21 Stuart Cres. **E16**
9 Stuart Gr. **E16**
9 Stuart Pk. **E16**
9 Stuart Sq. **E16**
9 Stuart Wynd **E16**
2 Student Centre **M16**
11 Succoth Av. **J16**
11 Succoth Ct. **J16**
11 Succoth Gdns. **J16**
11 Succoth Park **J16**
11 Succoth Pl. **J16**
21 Suffolk Rd. **N14**
21 Summer Bank **M17**
6 Summer Pl. **M18**
22 Summer Trees Ct. **O13**
8 Summerfield Gdns. **O18**
8 Summerfield Pl. **O18**
21 Summerhall **N15**
Summerhall Pl.* = Causewayside
21 Summerhall Sq. **N15**
7 Summerside Pl. **M19**
7 Summerside St. **M19**
12 Sunbury Mews **K16**
12 Sunbury Pl. **K16**
12 Sunbury St. **K16**
14 Sunnybank Pl. **O17**
14 Sunnybank Terr. **O17**
Surgeon Sq.* = Infirmary St.

2 Surgeons' Hall **N16**
Surrey Pl.* = Borthwick Pl.
Surrey Sq.* = Sutherland St.
12 Sutherland St. **K16**
28 Swan Spring Av. **L12**
28 Swanston Av. **L11**
28 Swanston Cr. **L11**
28 Swanston Dr. **L10**
28 Swanston Gdns. **L11**
28 Swanston Golf Course **K10**
28 Swanston Gr. **L11**
28 Swanston Gro. **L10**
28 Swanston Loan **L11**
28 Swanston Pk. **L11**
28 Swanston Pl. **L11**
28 Swanston Rd. **L11**
28 Swanston Row **L11**
28 Swanston Terr. **L11**
28 Swanston View **L11**
28 Swanston Way **L11**
Sycamore Gdns.* = Saughton Rd. N.
Sycamore Terr.* = Saughton Rd. N.
15 Sydney Park **Q17**
15 Sydney Pl. **Q17**
15 Sydney Terr. **Q17**
13 Sylvan Pl. **M15**
21 Synagogue **N15**

22 Talisman Pl. **O13**
6 Tanfield **M18**
6 Tanfield La. **M18**
21 Tantallon Pl. **N15**
1 Tarvit St. **L15**
20 Tay St. **K15**
7 Taylor Gdns. **N19**
14 Taylor Pl. **O17**
19 Telephone House **J15**
12 Telfer Subway **K15**
5 Telford Coll. of Further Education **K18**
5 Telford Dr. **J18**
5 Telford Gdns. **J18**
5 Telford Pl. **J18**
5 Telford Rd. **J17**
20 Temple Park Cr. **K15**
9 Templeland Gro. **F16**
9 Templeland Rd. **F16**
7 Tennant St. **N18**
2 Teviot Pl. **M16**
2 Teviot Row **M16**
23 Teviotbank House **R14**
12 Teviotdale Pl. **L17**
21 Thirlestane La. **M14**
21 Thirlestane Rd. **M15**
Thistle Ct.* = Thistle St.
23 Thistle Foundation Homes **Q14**
12 Thistle Pl. **L15**
1 Thistle St. **M17**
1 Thistle St. La., N.E. **M17**
1 Thistle St. La.,N.W. **M17**
1 Thistle St. La., S.E. **M17**
1 Thistle St. La.,S.W. **M17**
19 Thomas Clouston Clinic **K13**
7 Thomas Fraser Ct. **N19**
25 Thomson Cr. **E11**
25 Thomson Dr. **E11**
25 Thomson Gro. **E11**
25 Thomson Rd. **E11**
Thomson's Ct.* = Grassmarket
27 Thorburn Gro. **J11**
27 Thorburn Rd. **H11**
7 Thorntree St. **O18**
8 Thornville Terr. **O18**
1 Thornybauk **L15**

7 Timber Bush **O19**
7 Tinto Pl. **N18**
20 Tipperlinn Rd. **L14**
Tobago Pl.* = Morrison St.
7 Tolbooth Wynd **N19**
1 Tollcross Sch. **L15**
26 Torduff Rd. **H10**
26 Torduff Res. **G10**
1 Torphichen Pl. **L16**
1 Torphichen St. **L16**
26 Torphin Hill Golf Course **G10**
26 Torphin Rd. **G11**
9 Torrance Park **F17**
7 Tower Pl. **O19**
7 Tower St. **O19**
7 Tower St. La. **O19**
16 Towerbank Sch. **R17**
7 Town Hall, Leith **N19**
7 Town Hall, Portobello **R16**
7 Trafalgar La. **N19**
7 Trafalgar St. **N19**
10 Traquair Park E. **G15**
10 Traquair Park W. **G15**
13 Traverse Theatre **M16**
6 Trinity Acad. **M19**
7 Trinity Acad. Annexe **N19**
6 Trinity Ct. **L19**
6 Trinity Cr. **L19**
6 Trinity Gro. **L19**
6 Trinity Rd. **L19**
7 Trinity Sch. (Primary) **(M19**
2 Tron Sq. **M16**
26 Turlies, The **H12**
Turnbull's Entry* = Potterrow
9 Turnhouse Rd. **D16**
23 Tweedsmuir House **R14**
18 Tyler's Acre Av. **G15**
18 Tyler's Acre Gdns. **G15**
18 Tyler's Acre Rd. **G15**
Tynecastle Bdgs.* = McLeod St.
11 Tynecastle La. **K15**
Tynecastle Pl.* = Gorgie Rd.
11 Tynecastle Sch. **K15**
19 Tynecastle Sch. Annexe **J15**
Tynecastle Terr.* = Gorgie Rd.

14 Ulster Cr. **P16**
14 Ulster Dr. **P16**
14 Ulster Gdns. **P16**
14 Ulster Gro. **P16**
14 Ulster Terr. **P16**
Union Ct* = Richmond Pl.
2 Union Pl. **N17**
2 Union St. **N17**
2 University Library **M15**
2 Univ. of Edinburgh **M16**
13 Upper Bow **M16**
11 Upper Coltbridge Terr. **K16**
3 Upper Cramond Ct. **E18**
12 Upper Dean Terr. **L17**
12 Upper Gilmore Pl. **L15**
12 Upper Gilmore Terr. **L15**
21 Upper Gray St. **N15**
1 Upper Grove Pl. **L15**
1 Usher Hall **L15**
21 Usher Institute **M15**

12 Valleyfield St. **L15**
7 Vanburgh Pl. **O18**
15 Vandeleur Av. **Q17**
15 Vandeleur Gro. **Q17**
15 Vandeleur Pl. **Q17**
12 Veitch's Sq. **L17**
1 Vennel **M16**
22 Ventnor Pl. **O14**

45

21 Ventnor Terr. **N14**
Vernon Cotts.* = Pittville St. La.
24 Vexhim Park **R15**
9 Victor Park Terr. **F16**
7 Victoria Park **M19**
7 Victoria Sch. **M20**
13 Victoria St. **M16**
13 Viewcraig Gdns. **N16**
13 Viewcraig St. **N16**
26 Viewfield Rd. **G12**
20 Viewforth **L15**
20 Viewforth Gdns. **L15**
20 Viewforth Sq. **L15**
20 Viewforth Terr. **L15**
Violet Bank* = Spring Gdns.
20 Violet Terr. **K15**
4 Vivian Terr. **G18**

7 Waddell Pl. **N18**
15 Wakefield Av. **Q17**
1 Walker St. **L16**
12 Walker Terr. **L16**
22 Walter Scott Av. **O13**
6 Wardie Av. **L19**
6 Wardie Cr. **L19**
6 Wardie Gro. **K19**
Wardie House La.* = Boswall Rd.
6 Wardie Park **L19**
6 Wardie Rd. **L19**
6 Wardie Sch. **L19**
6 Wardie Sq. **L19**
6 Wardie Steps **L19**
6 Wardieburn Dr. **K19**
5 Wardieburn Pl. E. **K19**
5 Wardieburn Pl. N. **K19**
5 Wardieburn Pl. S. **K19**
5 Wardieburn Pl. W. **K19**
5 Wardieburn Rd. **K19**
5 Wardieburn St. E. **K19**
5 Wardieburn St. W. **K19**
5 Wardieburn Terr. **K19**
19 Wardlaw Pl. **K15**
19 Wardlaw St. **K15**
19 Wardlaw Terr. **K15**
21 Warrender Park Cr. **L15**
21 Warrender Park Rd. **M15**
21 Warrender Park Terr. **M15**
6 Warriston Av. **M18**
6 Warriston Cem. **M18**
2 Warriston Cl.* = High St.
6 Warriston Cr. **M18**
6 Warriston Crem. **M18**
6 Warriston Dr. **L18**
6 Warriston Gdns. **L18**
6 Warriston Gro. **L18**
6 Warriston Pl. **M18**
6 Warriston Rd. **M19**
6 Warriston Terr. **L18**
12 Washington La. **K15**
12 Washington St. **K15**
7 Water St. **O19**
2 Waterloo Pl. **M17**
Water's Cl.* = Shore
21 Watertoun Rd. **N14**
20 Watson Cr. **K15**
23 Wauchope Av. **Q14**
23 Wauchope Cr. **Q14**
23 Wauchope House **Q14**
23 Wauchope Pl. **Q14**
23 Wauchope Rd. **Q14**
23 Wauchope Sq. **Q14**
23 Wauchope Terr. **Q14**
2 Waverley Bridge **M16**
2 Waverley Market **M16**
14 Waverley Park **M16**
14 Waverley Park Terr. **O17**
14 Waverley Pl. **O17**
2 Waverley Sta. **M16**

2 Waverley Steps **M16**
Wax Museum* = High St.
25 Weaver's Knowe Cr. **D11**
Websters Land* = West Port
18 Weir Ct. **F13**
12 Well Ct. **L16**
7 Wellington Pl. **O18**
2 Wellington St. **N17**
1 Wemyss Pl. **L17**
Wemys Pl. Mews* = Wemyss Pl.
13 West Adam St. **N16**
13 West Annandale St. **M18**
12 West Approach Rd. **L16**
13 West Bow **M16**
7 West Bowling Green St. **N19**
15 West Brighton Cr. **R16**
20 West Bryson Rd. **K15**
28 West Caïystane Rd. **L11**
26 West Carnethy Av. **H11**
20 West Castle Rd. **L15**
11 West Catherine Pl. **K16**
11 West Coates **K16**
11 West Ct. Ravelston **J17**
23 West Ct. Niddrie **Q14**
9 West Craigs Av. **D15**
9 West Craigs Cr. **E15**
7 West Cromwell St. **N19**
13 West Crosscauseway **N15**
1 West End **L16**
12 West End Pl. **K15**
12 West Fountain Pl. **K15**
West Grange Gdns.* = Grange Loan
5 West Granton Cr. **H19**
5 West Granton Dr. **J19**
5 West Granton Gdns. **J19**
5 West Granton Gr. **H19**
5 West Granton Gro. **J19**
5 West Granton Loan **J19**
5 West Granton Pl. **H19**
5 West Granton Rd. **J19**
5 West Granton Row **J19**
5 West Granton Terr. **J19**
5 West Granton View **J19**
5 West Harbour Rd. **K20**
21 West Mains Rd. **N13**
5 West Maitland St. **L16**
21 West Mayfield **N14**
West Mill La.* = Dean Path
26 West Mill Rd. **G11**
21 West Newington Pl. **N15**
2 West Nicolson St. **N16**
2 West Norton Pl. **N17**
12 West Park Pl. **K15**
5 West Pilton Av. **J18**
5 West Pilton Bank **H19**
5 West Pilton Circus **J19**
5 West Pilton Circus Pk. **J19**
5 West Pilton Cr. **H19**
5 West Pilton Crossway **J19**
5 West Pilton Gdns. **J19**
5 West Pilton Gro. **J19**
5 West Pilton Park (street) **J19**
5 West Pilton Pk. **J18**
5 West Pilton Pl. **J19**
5 West Pilton Rise **J19**
5 West Pilton Rd. **J19**
5 West Pilton St. **J19**
5 West Pilton Terr. **J19**
5 West Pilton View **J18**
1 West Port **M16**
1 West Port House **M16**
21 West Preston St. **N15**
1 West Princes St. Gdns. **M16**

1 West Register House **L16**
2 West Register St. **M17**
21 West Relugas Rd. **M14**
2 West Richmond St. **N16**
21 West Savile Rd. **N14**
21 West Saville Terr. **N14**
5 West Shore Rd. **H20**
12 West Silvermills La. **L17**
1 West Tollcross **L15**
5 West Winnelstrae **K18**
5 West Woods **K18**
15 Westbank Ln. **R17**
15 Westbank Pl. **R17**
15 Westbank St. **R17**
25 Westburn Av. **F12**
25 Westburn Gdns. **F12**
25 Westburn Gro. **F12**
25 Westburn Park **F12**
17 Westburn Sch. **F13**
17 Wester Broom Av. **F15**
17 Wester Broom Dr. **F15**
17 Wester Broom Gdns. **F15**
17 Wester Broom Gro. **F15**
17 Wester Broom Pl. **F15**
17 Wester Broom Terr. **F15**
11 Wester Coates Av. **K16**
12 Wester Coates Gdns. **K16**
11 Wester Coates Rd. **K16**
11 Wester Coates Terr. **K16**
19 Wester Craiglockhart Hill **J13**
5 Wester Drylaw Av. **H18**
5 Wester Drylaw Dr. **H18**
5 Wester Drylaw Gdns. **H18**
5 Wester Drylaw Paddock **H18**
5 Wester Drylaw Pk. **J18**
5 Wester Drylaw Pl. **H18**
5 Wester Drylaw Row **J17**
25 Wester Hailes Centre **F12**
26 Wester Hailes Dr. **F12**
17 Wester Hailes Education Centre **F13**
26 Wester Hailes Park **G12**
17 Wester Hailes Rd. **F13**
Western Corner* = Saughtonhall Dr.
11 Western Gdns. **J16**
11 Western General Hosp. **K18**
11 Western Pl. **J16**
11 Western Terr. **J16**
19 Westfield Av. **J15**
19 Westfield Court **J15**
19 Westfield St. **J15**
26 Westgarth Av. **H11**
20 Westhall Gdns. **L15**
Westland Cotts.* = Ravenscroft Pl.
Westland Houses* = Ravenscroft Pl.
19 Wheatfield Pl. **J15**
19 Wheatfield Rd. **J15**
19 Wheatfield St. **K15**
19 Wheatfield Terr. **J15**
19 Whinhill Pk. **G14**
19 White Park **K15**
24 Whitehill Rd. **S14**
24 Whitehill St **S14**
Whitehorse Cl.* = Canongate
21 Whitehouse Loan **L15**
3 Whitehouse Rd. **E18**
· 21 Whitehouse Terr. **M14**
19 Whitson Cr. **H15**
19 Whitson Gro. **H15**
19 Whitson Pl. E. **H15**
19 Whitson Pl. W. **H15**
19 Whitson Rd. **H15**
19 Whitson Terr. **H15**
19 Whitson Walk **H15**
19 Whitson Way **H15**

14 Whyte Pl. **O17**
14 Wilfred Terr. **P17**
1 William St. **L16**
1 William St. La., N.E. **L16**
1 William St. La., N.W. **L16**
1 William St. La., S.E. **L16**
1 William St. La., S.W. **L16**
Williamfield* = Rosefield Av.
7 Willowbank Row **M19**
14 Willowbrae Av. **P16**
14 Willowbrae Gdns. **P16**
14 Willowbrae Rd. **P16**
14 Willowbrae Sch. **P16**
19 Willowpark St. **J15**
16 Wilson's Park **R17**
21 Wilton Rd. **N13**
Windmill La* = Buccleuch Pl.
16 Windsor Pl. **R16**
17 Windsor St. **N17**
13 Windsor St. La. **N17**
28 Winton Dr. **M10**
28 Winton Gro. **L11**
28 Winton Loan **M10**
28 Winton Pk. **L10**
28 Winton Terr. **L10**
14 Wishaw Terr. **O17**
23 Wisp Green **R14**
24 Wisp, The **R14**
29 Wolrige Rd. **O12**
14 Wolseley Cr. **P17**
Wolseley Gdns.* = Wolseley Cr.
Wolseley Pl.* = Wolseley Cr.
14 Wolseley Terr. **P17**
20 Wood Pl. **L14**
8 Woodbine Terr. **O18**
21 Woodburn House **M14**
Woodburn Pl.* = Canaan La.
20 Woodburn Terr. **L14**
26 Woodfield Av. **G11**
26 Woodfield Pk **G11**
26 Woodhall Av. **F11**
26 Woodhall Bank **G11**
26 Woodhall Dr. **F11**
26 Woodhall Gro. **G11**
26 Woodhall Rd. **G11**
25 Woodhall Terr. **F11**
15 Woodlands Gro. **Q15**
16 Woodside Terr. **S16**
22 Woodstock Pl. **O13**
8 Woodville Terr. **O18**
31 Woolmet Cr. **R12**
13 Wright's Houses **L15**

7 Yardheads **N19**
12 Yeaman La. **L15**
12 Yeaman Pl. **K15**
29 Yewlands Cr. **O12**
29 Yewlands Gdns. **O12**
Yoole Pl.* = Pipe St.
York Bdgs* = Queen St.
2 York La. **M17**
7 York Pl. **M17**
6 York Rd. **M19**
1 Young St. **L16**
1 Young St. La., N. **L16**
1 Young St. La., S. **L16**

6 Zetland Pl. **L19**
10 Zoo **G16**